D1262

Military Headdress

Military Headdress

A pictorial history of
military headgear from
1660 to 1914

Colonel Robert H. Rankin

**British Guard's
lmet, c. 1817.** This is
e of the rarer and
ore beautiful helmets
he British Life Guards
ttern of 1817. The
ull and comb are of
vered metal with gilt
ings. The large gilt
f-sunburst plate
ars the Royal Arms,
gether with the battle
nours. The highly
corated chin scales
d lion's-head bosses
e of gilt. Gilt leaves
corate the back and
es of the skull. The
st is of black
arskin. This helmet
y have been the
piration for the
met of the First City
op of Philadelphia,
nsylvania,
strated in Plate 56.
allis & Wallis.)

LONDON: ARMS & ARMOUR PRESS
NEW YORK: HIPPOCRENE BOOKS, INC

Published in 1976 by
Arms and Armour Press,
Lionel Leventhal Limited,
2-6 Hampstead High Street,
London NW3 1PR

ISBN 0 85368 310 7

Published in the United States 1976
by HIPPOCRENE BOOKS, INC.
171 Madison Avenue
New York, N.Y. 10016

Library of Congress Catalog Card
Number 75-43821
ISBN 0-88254-341-7

Printed in Great Britain by
T. & A. Constable Ltd., Edinburgh

Acknowledgments
In preparing this account of military
headdress I have received the
wholehearted cooperation of many
individuals who have most
generously assisted me in making
photographs and research materials
available.

Kimball P. Vickery supplied many
of the photographs and lent his advice
as an advanced collector and
historian. The late Norm Hobson
freely supplied photographs and
information concerning his extensive
collection. His wife, Mrs. Flora
Hobson, made additional materials
available. N. R. Belmont-Maitland
and David Scheinmann, Tradition
Ltd., 188 Piccadilly, London, W.1.
made many photographs and other
material available, and gave
permission for their use. Richard K.
Riehn, The Soldier Shop, an expert
on European military uniforms, gave
valued advice. David Ross, Curator,
Human History Collections,
Manitoba Museum of Man and
Nature, contributed much on the
Canadian Army and Militia. Herman
Otten, General Manager, Wallis &
Wallis, 210 High Street, Lewes,
Sussex, cooperated in making
photographs available and arranged
with Wallis & Wallis for their
publication. Norm Flayderman also
contributed photographs as well as
making his extensive military
reference library available. Donald
E. Kloster, Assistant Curator,
Division of Military History, The
Smithsonian Institution, contributed
from his vast knowledge of United
States Army and Militia uniforms.
George A. Petersen, Replica Models,
Inc. supplied considerable
information on European headdress.

Thanks are also due to Miss Betti
Sprigg, Audio-Visual Division, U.S.
Department of Defense; Michael J.
McAfee, Curator, West Point
Museum; Miss Sheilagh S. Jameson,
Archivist, Glenbow-Alberta
Institute; J. R. Leconte, Le
Conservateur en Chef, and J.
Lorette, Le Conservateur-Adjoint,
Musée Royal de l'Armée, Brussels;
Lieutenant General Alfred
Rosenbaum, Belgian Army
(Retired); Peter Hlinka; William
Guthman, Horace Mann, Curator,
U.S. Army Quartermaster Museum,
Joseph Hefter; W. C. Turpin,
Curator, The War Memorial
Museum of Virginia; and Olle
Cederloff, Director, Karin
Oscarsson, Librarian, Svante Ison
Warfvinge and Jorgen Lindkvist, all
of the Royal Army Museum,
Stockholm.

To Dr and Mrs Rome Rankin

List of Contents

132: British officer's helmet, Leicestershire Regiment, 1881–1901: *79*
133: Mexican officer's Pickelhaube, c. 1890: *80*
134: Netherlands other rank's dress helmet, Royal Marine Corps, post-1896: *80*
135: Swedish other rank's Pickelhaube, c. 1900: *81*
136: British Home Service 1878-pattern, Royal Marine Artillery, c. 1901: *81*
137: British officer's Home Service Helmet, Cheshire Regiment, post-1901: *82*
138: German officer's Pickelhaube, Queen Olga's Dragoons (1st Württemburg) No. 25, early 1900s: *82*
139: Baden infantry officer's helmet, early 1900s: *83*
140: Mexican officer's Pickelhaube, post-1905: *83*
141: German other rank's artillery helmet, Mecklenburg Artillery, c. 1910: *83*
142: German officer's Pickelhaube with white plume, 1st Baden Life Guard Grenadiers (No. 109), c. 1914: *84*
143: German bandmaster's helmet, 78th Field Artillery Regiment (8th Saxon), c. 1912: *84*
144: Prussian other rank's Pickelhaube, c. 1914: *85*
145: Russian Guard cuirassier Pickelhaube, c. 1914: *85*

6. Grenadier caps and bearskins: *86*
146: Prussian officer's grenadier cap (Grenadiermutze), 32nd Grenadier Regiment, c. 1760: *86*
147: British officer's mitre cap, Grenadier Company, 43rd Foot, c. 1740–9: *87*
148: British officer's Racoon-skin cap, Royal Fusiliers, c. 1890: *88*
149: Austrian other rank's grenadier cap, c. 1830: *88*
150: Prussian other rank's grenadier cap (front view), 1st Foot Guards,

151: Prussian other rank's grenadier cap (side view), 1st Foot Guard, 1894 pattern: *89*

7. The mirleton and busby: *90*
152: Prussian Flugelmutze, von Ruesch or 'Black' Hussar Regiment, c. 1750s: *90*
153: Netherlands horse artillery officer's busby, c. 1870: *90*
154: British officer's busby, Royal Artillery, 1856–78: *90*
155: British other rank's envelope busby, Rifle Brigade, c. 1890: *91*
156: British officer's busby, 15th Hussars, c. 1890: *91*
157: United States busby, New York Hussars, c. 1890–1900: *91*
158: Prussian officer's busby, 1st (Lieb) Hussars, c. 1900: *92*
159: British other rank's busby, Middlesex Yeomanry, c. 1900: *93*
160: Russian infantry officer's busby, c. 1900: *93*
161: United States drum major's busby, Marine Corps Band (The President's Own), c. 1912: *93*

8. The Lancer cap: *94*
162: French Czapka of the 8th Chevau-Legers Lanciers Polonais, c. 1812: *94*
163: British officer's lancer cap, 9th Lancers, 1832– c. 1856: *94*
164: United States lancer cap, c. 1840: *94*
165: Russian lancer cap (Czapka), Imperial 14th Lancer Regiment, c. 1840–55: *95*
166: Prussian officer's lancer cap (Czapka), 3rd Uhlan Regiment, Emperor Alexander of Russia's Uhlans (1st Brandenburg), c. 1844–62: *95*
167: French other rank's lancer cap (Czapka), c. 1857: *96*
168, 169 and **170:** Officer's lightweight headdress, post-1850: *96*
171: Polish lancer cap (Czapka), c. 1880: *97*

172: British other rank's lancer cap, 12th Lancer, c. 1900: *98*
173: British officer's lancer cap, 17th Lancers, post-1883: *99*
174: German other rank's lancer cap, Kaiser Wilhelm I Uhlans (2nd Württemburg) No. 20, c. 1900: *99*
175: British officer's lancer cap, 9th Lancers, post-1901: *100*
176: Prussian Uhlan officer's lancer cap (Czapka), c. 1910: *100*
177: Austrian officer's lancer cap (Czapka), 3rd Uhlan Regiment, c. 1910: *100*
178: Prussian other rank's lancer cap (Czapka), 1st Guard Uhlan Regiment, c. 1910–17: *101*
179: Polish other rank's lancer cap (Czapka), c. 1914: *101*

9. Tropical helmets: *102*
180: United States general officer's dress helmet, c. 1860: *102*
181: Indian Army officer's tropical helmet, c. 1880: *103*
182: United States enlisted man's summer helmet, Model 1880: *103*
183: Indian Army other rank's headdress, c. 1890: *104*
184: United States militia cork helmet, c. 1890–1900: *104*
185: South African artillery officer's helmet, c. 1895: *104*
186: British other rank's sun helmet, c. 1898: *105*
187: United States Army sun helmet, c. 1900: *105*
188: British other rank's tropical helmet, Civil Service Volunteer Rifle Corps, c. 1901–08: *106*
189: German other rank's tropical helmet, c. 1914: *106*
190: German infantry tropical helmet, c. 1914: *107*
191: German officer's tropical helmet, c. 1914: *107*
192: German infantry other rank's tropical helmet, c. 1914: *108*
193: German tropical helmet, c. 1914: *109*
194: Belgian non-commissioned

Introduction

Of all the various components of military uniform, headdress is perhaps of greatest interest to collectors. One important reason for this is that an item of military headdress is a complete unit in itself, comparatively easy to display and requiring a minimum of care. Fortunately for historians and collectors, since military headdresses are usually made of leather or metal, they have survived when other parts of the uniform have fallen prey to time and moths, or have been worn out through subsequent conversion to civilian use. In the absence of written regulations on the subject, the survival of headdress is very important, for it provides accurate, first-hand historical information which simply is not available for other parts of military uniform.

Since earliest times men have worn some distinctive form of head covering to identify themselves as members of a military unit. Sometimes this would have been merely a coloured plume or a bunch of ribbons attached to a conventional civilian hat. Alternatively, it might have been a special kind of headdress such as a helmet or a shako, perhaps bearing an additional distinguishing device such as plumes, ribbons, tassels or front plate. In America, such a headdress was sometimes the only item of uniform boasted by soldiers of the poorer militia units.

In developing the story of military headdress, it is on occasion difficult to date exactly the introduction of a particular type. A given style was not always worn continuously by the army of a particular nation but might be set aside for a while and reappear later. Nor would different nations necessarily adopt a style simultaneously. Furthermore, a particular military fashion might be retained by one or more countries long after it had been discarded by the nation of origin. Therefore, for purposes of this review, any dates given are approximate.

The origins of military uniform are customarily dated to somewhere around the late 1600s. Apparently the first military head covering was simply an adaptation of a civilian hat, and it is with this hat that we begin our present study. The story virtually ends around 1914 when so-called modern warfare put an end to the colourful uniforms of former times. Within that period of a little more than two centuries, military headdress went through several cycles of development, exhibiting fashions that were sometimes ornate in the extreme.

In a review of military headdress, it is interesting to note the influence which some nations exerted upon others. The 'Pickelhaube' of the Prussian service is a good example of this. Copied not only by other German 'lander' (states), it was also borrowed in one form or another by many foreign nations, including England, Austria, Sweden, the United States, Mexico, Colombia and Bolivia. The Pickelhaube was introduced in 1842, and in due course various modifications appeared. The ball top in lieu of the spike was adopted for artillery in 1846. Early models of this helmet had an extremely high crown, characteristic of the military headdress of that era. Later models had successively lower crowns with modified peaks and spikes. For parade (gala) a black or white plume ('Busch') was worn instead of the spike or ball ornament with the exception of musicians who wore red. In the case of officers and some other ranks, these plumes were of hair. General officers wore a feather plume, white and black for Prussian generals, blue and white for Bavarian generals, red and black for Württemburg generals, etc. For gala certain elite units wore a metal helmet with some form of an eagle or lion instead of the plume.

Some military historians affirm that the spiked helmet was actually conceived by Tsar Nicholas I of Russia and that Frederick William IV of Prussia saw a prototype while visiting the Russian monarch. It is related that he liked it so much that upon his return home he immediately adopted it for his own troops. It was not until 1848 that Nicholas ordered it for the Russian army.

The trencher-topped lancer cap or 'czapka' is of Polish origin. It was introduced into the French service in 1807 by Napoleon and was soon adopted thereafter in various modifications by Austria, Russia, Germany, Sweden, England, Mexico and other nations. Interestingly enough, it was not adopted by the United States Regular Army, although that army did derive military fashions from England and Europe. However, a limited number of militia units in the United States wore it for a time. This cap originated in an ancient four-sided soft cap with a peak known as a 'konfederatka', which was worn by Polish peasants.

As noted previously, following the introduction of uniforms during the latter part of the seventeenth century, the earliest type of military headdress was simply a civilian hat. This had a low crown and a broad brim. The broad brim proved a handicap to free military movement, and consequently it was turned up on one side. Later it was turned up on two sides to form the 'bicorne' or on three sides to make a 'tricorne', both popular throughout the eighteenth century.

The bicornes and tricornes used by soldiers were decorated around the edges with tape of various colours. In the case of officers this trim was often in gold or silver material. Tassels, cockades and plumes also distinguished the military types. As in the case of all military headdress, the more gorgeous the trimmings, the higher the rank.

The 'chapeau' or cocked hat is a refinement of the bicorne, being turned up on two sides and lavishly trimmed with cockades and plumes. In America those that could be compressed and carried under the arm were known as 'chapeaux-de-bras', while those of a rigid form were known simply as chapeaux. These cocked hats were most often worn 'fore and aft' or cocked over one eye. In a few instances they were worn from 'side to side'. For a time during the early 1800s, in most armies, the chapeau de bras became absurdly large, the baseline being curved to such an extent that the ends almost touched the shoulders when the head was turned. It is of some interest to note that, even after this headdress was abandoned for issue to other ranks, it was retained until comparatively recently for dress wear by general and staff officers.

The fur busby appeared as early as the second half of the seventeenth century. It was worn by artillery units as well as by hussars. A late nineteenth-century version was adopted by certain elite English rifle units who, by virtue of their ability to manoeuvre rapidly, likened themselves to foot cavalry and wore a modified hussar uniform.

Around the beginning of the 1700s the so-called grenadier cap appeared. It has been suggested that this particular type of headdress originated because the hat with a brim interfered with the overhand movement of the grenadier in throwing his grenade. Some experts, however, point out that the grenade was most often thrown with an underhand movement and claim that this cap was introduced to allow the musket to be more easily slung over the shoulder. In any event, the cap was at first made of cloth with a semi-stiff cloth front turned up in such a manner that a badge or other identifying device could be displayed. This insignia was embroidered. The cap itself was at times low in profile and at other times long enough to fall over on one side. It gradually developed into a tall cloth or fur cap attached to a large metal front plate bearing an identifying device which was usually quite elaborate.

Grenadiers were specially selected men of considerable strength and courage, and were considered superior to most troops. As the need for their proficiency disappeared, the grenadier cap was retained in some armies for wear by elite units.

About the mid-1700s a high conical cap with a long loose flap which could be wound up about the cap or allowed to hang loose was introduced. Known in Germany as a 'Flugelmutze' or 'Schackelhue', and in France as a 'mirliton' it soon became popular for mounted troops, particularly hussars, in a number of armies, including those of England, the German states, Russia, France and Sweden.

Towards the end of the 1700s the 'Tarleton' helmet or jockey cap appeared. This was a leather cap with a front peak, and was usually decorated with a fur crest. In some instances this crest ran from a distinguishing plate in front, across the crown and down the back of the cap, but in other versions it had no cap plate and the crest extended from the base of the peak, up over the crown and down the back. Still other versions had a fur crest placed across the crown from side to side.

During the closing years of the eighteenth century (some authorities fix the date as 1769) the 'Kaskett' was introduced into the Austrian service. This was a round leather cap with a flat top and a rounded flap turned back up against the front. This flap provided the background for an embossed metal identifying cap plate which was irregular in outline and had a raised border. At first this plate bore the Imperial cypher but after 1790 it displayed the Austrian double-headed eagle. The Imperial colours of yellow and black appeared in a wool tuft which decorated the left side of this headdress.

The 'shako', derived from a Magyar word for 'peaked cap', was perhaps the most universally adopted of all military headdresses. It appears to have originated in Austria when the flat-top cylindrical cap then being worn by Magyar troops in the Austrian Frontier Force was modified in 1796 by the addition of a front peak. The shako underwent many changes and was adopted by most armies. It was introduced into the British and French services around 1800, followed by the German states and the rest of Europe, as well as the United States.

The shako gradually became lower than it was in its original form, but had a front piece projecting above the crown. The so-called bell-top shako, with the top much wider than the bottom, then replaced it in popularity.

This particular type was first used extensively by Prussia. Around the mid-1800s a return was made, notably in the British, French and Austrian armies, to the early flat-top cylindrical style, but of medium height and with both front and rear peaks. It became still lower and had a rounded back, a straight front angled slightly forward and a flat top. A variety of front plates were worn, depicting regimental devices, national arms and royal cyphers. The top front was adorned variously with coloured tufts, plumes and pompons. Chin chains, chin scales or even plain leather chin straps were used. Except for some Saxon units, the German states in the late 1800s wore a shako with a rounded back, front and rear peaks, a flat top and straight front.

Apart from the crested helmets already noted, there was a development of metal helmets decorated in the classical Greek and Roman manner, with a high metal crest which was either topped with fur or had a long trailing horsehair mane. This helmet often had a coloured plume on one side, and a coloured tuft of hair at the front of the crest. Decorative chin chains or scales were worn with this headdress. Used at first largely as a protective covering for the head, it later became less defensive. The helmet was made famous by Napoleon's cuirassiers and was adopted in many countries including Austria, England, France, Mexico and Brazil.

Peculiar to Scots regiments is the bonnet, a cap with a headband topped with a wide circular crown. It is decorated in various ways according to the regiment. With a wide headband topped by a framework covered with feathers it became known as the feather bonnet.

The high cylindrical hat with its narrow brim, popularly known in civilian life as a top hat, was in the early 1800s occasionally decorated with a plume, front plate, cockade, hackle or coloured wool tuft, or with a combination of these emblems. Hats of this type were worn at one time by most armies.

Near the mid-1800s a stiff felt shako with inward-sloping sides and flat top smaller than the bottom, was introduced for the use of French troops in Africa. Called a 'casquette', this headdress evolved into the 'kepi', a small cap with soft cloth sides and stiff, forward-sloping top. Both casquette and kepi had a flat leather peak. The kepi was popular not only in France but was also worn extensively by both the Federal and Confederate troops in the American Civil War.

The field cap, also known variously as the barracks cap, quarters cap, fatigue cap or forage cap, probably first appeared in the early 1800s. It is usually a cloth cap with or without a peak. It varies greatly in different armies but is, broadly speaking, characterised by utility, comfort and convenience.

A semi-soft, wide-brimmed slouch hat, brown in colour, turned up on one side, and often referred to as a bush hat, was

2: United States Militia officer's chapeau-de-bras, with storage case, c. 1815.
This interesting and unusual set was the property of a New York State militia officer. The hat is of brownish-black felt with a stamped black leather cockade at the top. At the bottom centre is a small silvered American eagle. Four gilt cords connect the cockade and the eagle and small gilt tassels hang from the points of the headdress. Above it extends a white plume. The cardboard storage box is covered with figured wallpaper in red, white, blue, brown, black and yellow. (Guthman Collection.)

introduced into the British service towards the end of the nineteenth century, when it was issued to volunteer troops from the colonies. The hat would be decorated with the unit's insignia and at times with a wide coloured hat-band or 'puggree'. At about the same time, a similar hat in grey felt was introduced for Imperial German troops serving in Africa. The brim edging and hat band were coloured or white. The right side of the brim was turned up and was fastened to the crown of the hat by a black, white and red cockade. After 1900 the bush hat became standard wear for troops from Australia and New Zealand.

A somewhat similar hat became popular with both Federal and Confederate troops during the American Civil War. This was of black felt and in some instances was turned up on the left side, where it was fastened to the crown by a decorative device of an eagle and stars. Plumes usually adorned such a hat. A double hat cord, ending in acorns, was worn. For general officers both cord and acorns were gold. Lower-ranking officers wore a gold and black silk cord, and other ranks a worsted cord in the colour or colours of their branch of service. The front of the hat bore a distinguishing badge, i.e., 'U.S.' for general officers, and combinations of wreaths and branch-of-service devices for other officers. Other ranks simply displayed the branch-of-service device. A similar hat was worn during the Indian wars in the American West.

In 1885 a new hat was introduced in the United States for field duty. This was commonly known as the field hat or campaign hat. It was characteristic of American troops for many years. This wide-brimmed olive drab hat was creased front to rear. In general the hat cord was like that of the hat of the American Civil War. No distinguishing device was worn on the front. In the early 1900s the shape of the hat was changed by blocking the crown with four dimples and was called a 'Montana peak', in fancied resemblance to a mountain peak. At the same time the brim was changed from semi-stiff to stiff. This hat was always popular with other ranks in the United States Army and the Marine Corps. The hat cord was similar to that previously worn for the Army. Marine general officers wore a gold cord and acorns and other officers wore a scarlet silk and gold cord. Military planners ruled that this hat was not practical for modern warfare and today its use is restricted to such elite soldiers as drill sergeants.

A slouch or bush hat of light material became popular with British, American and Allied troops during the fighting in the South Pacific during the Second World War and was worn to some extent by U.S. troops fighting in Vietnam.

Sun or tropical helmets of cork or other material, covered with white or khaki cloth, appeared during the last half of the 1800s. Prior to that, headdress worn in warm climates was fitted with a white cloth cover.

Of growing interest to collectors, but generally difficult to find, are the various covers worn over headdress in inclement weather. Also commanding greater support are the containers in which the headdresses were shipped or stored. They comprise a field of special interest for the collector with an ample purse. A few of these items are pictured in these pages.

Obviously it is not possible to illustrate the many hundreds and even thousands of different items of headdress available in museums and in the hands of private collectors. Since this book is limited in size, an attempt has been made to picture and describe those items best showing the development of military headdress, together with examples likely to be of most interest to the average collector.

It is worth noting that in the United States services the term 'enlisted man', through the senior grades of sergeant, is generally equivalent to 'other rank' in the British and European armies.

Also, in the United States services, the term 'cap' is at times loosely applied to what in other armies is known as a 'shako', and the term 'visor' is applied to what is elsewhere known as the 'peak'.

In preparing this volume on military headdress, the various items have been arranged approximately in chronological sequence, but once again it must be emphasised that dates should only be used as rough guidelines.

1. The hat and its development into the cocked and slouched hats

3: United States Marine officer wearing cocked hat, c. 1776. The cocked hat worn by this officer of the period of the American Revolution is typical of its time. The hat is black with black trim about the edges. The cockade is also black with a gilt button. (Official U.S. Marine Corps Photograph.)

4: Swedish foot soldier's grey-felt hat, mid-seventeenth century. This hat is typical of the civilian-type hat first worn by uniformed troops. In service it was usually turned up on one side. Later it was turned up on three sides to form a tricorne, then on two sides to form the bicorne. The bicorne subsequently developed into the chapeau. (Royal Army Museum, Stockholm.)

5: United States officer's tricorne, c. 1776. One of the earliest forms of military headdress is the tricorne, made by turning up on three sides the broad brim of a civilian hat. Shown here is an American version, worn by Colonel Jonathan Pettibone, 18th Connecticut Militia, during the American Revolutionary War. It is fairly typical of the headdress worn by British, European and American armies of the period. This specimen is actually a transitional model between the civilian tricorne and the later, more compact military version. It is of black wool felt, with a small mixture of rabbit fur. The edges are bound with black silk. Black silk cockades decorate two sides of the hat. It is unlined but does have a glazed cotton sweatband. Other ranks' tricornes were often trimmed around the edges with coloured cloth binding and cockades, while officers often had gold cord and plumes. (The Smithsonian Institution.)

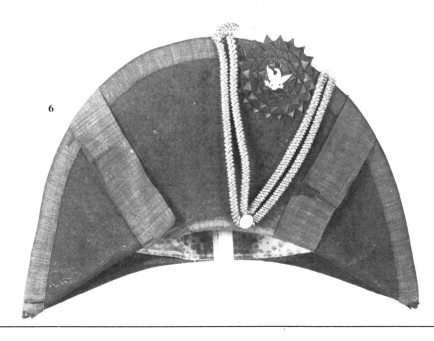

6: United States officer's cocked hat (chapeau), c. 1809–12. This general officer's hat is typical of this particular type of military headdress. It originated in the broad-brimmed civilian hat of the era, turned up on two sides, and went through many modifications. This specimen is made of heavy black beaver. As is customary, the front fold or cock is somewhat smaller than the back fold or fan. The edges are bound with black silk ribbon and two diagonal stripes of black silk form a 'V' effect on the front. A 'V' of gold bullion terminates in a gold button. The black leather cockade bears a small gold eagle, and behind it a leather plume-socket is attached. This hat is silk lined and has a leather sweatband. (The Smithsonian Institution.)

7: French marine's hat, c. 1800. An adaptation of the civilian top hat for military use. In this case the left part of the brim has been greatly enlarged and turned up against the hat itself. Of greenish felt, it has a black leather top. A cloth cockade and two ribbons decorate the top centre of the turned-up brim, and a brass fouled anchor decorates the centre section. A headdress such as this is extremely rare and seldom seen outside museums. (Musée Royal de l'Armée, Brussels.)

8: United States enlisted man's artillery hat, c. 1858. This hat was worn to some extent during the American Civil War. It is of black felt, with the brim turned up on the right side and held in place by a yellow-metal device in the form of the modified Arms of the U.S. Yellow-metal cannons decorate the front of the hat. A red double cord encircles the base of the crown, with its tassels in front, and a black feather appears on the left side of the crown. This hat was never very popular with the troops. (The Smithsonian Institution.)

10

9: United States enlisted man's campaign hat, c. 1872. This black felt campaign hat was something of an experimental item which was worn for only three years. It was reported to have been extremely uncomfortable and hot for summer wear, particularly in the plains and desert regions of the western United States. (The Smithsonian Institution.)

10: United States enlisted man's campaign hat, c. 1875. This is one of several models of black felt hats worn by the United States Army. The hat band is also black. Troops serving in the field on the Western Plains sometimes wore these hats in a variety of ways, such as turning the brim up in front and back, or turning the brim up on both sides to form a kind of bicorne. (The Smithsonian Institution.)

11. British surgeon's cocked hat, 1st Volunteer Battalion, Somerset Light Infantry, c. 1890. The vagaries of headdress worn by the regiments of the British Army were not followed by the regimental non-combatant staff – the surgeons, veterinary surgeons and chaplains – who always wore the cocked hat. Cocked hats were also worn by the officers of departmental corps and by general and staff officers. The 1900 Dress Regulations ordered that they be of black silk, the left side to be $6\frac{1}{4}$ inches high, the right side $5\frac{3}{4}$ inches, and each corner $4\frac{3}{8}$ inches long. On the right side was to be a black silk cockade, with a lace loop fastened by a button. At each corner there were bullion tassels, and midway between the loop and tassel, front and back, a band of $1\frac{3}{4}$-inch oak-leaf pattern black braid. The specimen shown belonged to Surgeon/Captain R. J. H. Scott, and has silver lace and a red and white feather plume. Scott served from 1883 to 1893. (Wallis & Wallis.)

11

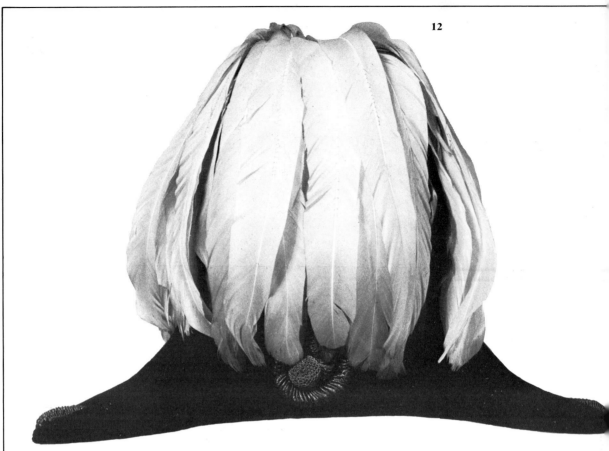

12

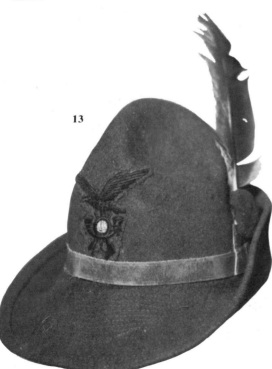

13

12: Canadian general officer's full dress cocked hat, c. 1900. The ha[...] of fine-quality black beaver, decorated with gold lace and tassels. T[...] plume consists of white swan feathers over scarlet feathers. A simil[...] cocked hat was worn by general officers in most armies at this perio[...] (Manitoba Museum of Man & Nature.)

13: Italian Alpini other rank's hat, c. 1910. This interesting item is [...] field green felt with the brim turned down in the front and up in the back. A russet green leather hat band surrounds the bottom of the body of the hat. On the front appears a black embroidered badge in form of a light infantry bugle-horn, over which is an eagle with outspread wings. In the centre of the badge appears a light green cl[...] disc upon which is a gilt-metal numeral '4'. An eagle feather, with a[...] dark blue pompon at the lower end, appears on the left side of the h[...] (Kimball P. Vickery Collection.)

14: United States enlisted man's Montana peak felt campaign hat, **1911.** This hat was so called because the crown, indented in four places, supposedly resembles a mountain peak. The hat band is oliv[...] drab cloth. Enlisted men wore a double cord round the hat band in [...] colour or colours of the wearer's arm or service. These cords end in[...] front of the hat with two acorns. Officers, other than generals, wor[...] hat cord and acorns of gold and black, while generals wore a gold c[...] and acorns. A regimental badge was sometimes worn in the front ventilation eyelet, and a cordovan leather chin strap was fitted. Un[...] States Marines wore a similar hat but referred to it as a field hat. Enlisted Marines wore no hat cords, but Marine officers wore cord[...] and acorns of gold and scarlet. This hat was a popular item with all ranks but it was phased out as impractical at the beginning of Worl[...] War Two. Today it has been adopted by both the United States Ar[...] and United States Marine Corps for certain designated individual enlisted men, particularly drill sergeants. (The Smithsonian Institution.)

14

15

**5: German officer's tropical hat,
. 1914.** This hat, worn in South
West Africa, is of grey felt with a
blue band and blue trim to the edge
of the brim. Colours were used to
identify the colonial area of the
German Empire in which the
wearer was stationed: blue, South
West Africa; red, Cameroons;
white, South East Africa. The brim
is turned up and held in place by a
stamped black, white and red
(Imperial) Kokarde. No State
(Land) Kokarde was worn since
these troops represented the whole
of Germany and not a particular
state. The hat is lined with silk.
(Norm Hobson Collection.)

16

**16: Italian sharpshooter's
(Bersaglieri) other rank's hat.** This
unique headdress is of stiff black
felt with a covering of thin black
leather on the brim and
approximately half-way up on the
body. On a red, white and green
cockade appears a brass badge in
the form of a light infantry bugle-
horn superimposed upon crossed
rifles. In the centre of the badge
appears a flaming grenade with a
black-enamelled cross on it. A
plume of dark green cocks'
feathers decorates the right side of
the hat. This item is rather rare.
(Kimball P. Vickery Collection.)

2. Shakos and kepis

17

17: United States bell-top shako, c. 1810–15. The shako, belonging to a now-unknown militia unit, is of heavy black leather with fairly narrow, flat black leather peak or visor. A narrow flap turns up round the rear half of the cap. The slightly domed top is decorated with a gilt tassel and a yellow feather plume appears at the top front. The front of the shako is hand painted in red, gold and brown, to form the words 'Volunteer Guards' in a half-arc about a crudely executed eagle and seven five-pointed stars. A brass star is attached to the lower front of the shako. (Guthman Collection.)

18: British shako, c. 1812. The so-called Waterloo shako of the pattern introduced into the British army c. 1812 is of black felt with black leather peak, and is distinguished by the raised front which extends above the top of the body. The front plate is a gilt cartouche with a raised edge and a crown. In the centre of the plate are the letters 'GR' (Georgius Rex). Decorative gold cord is draped across the front in the form of an inverted 'V', and gold tassels hang from the right side. At the top left side is a red and white plume. (Wallis & Wallis.)

19: French officer's shako, 54th Regiment of Infantry, c. 1812. The shako, allegedly an adaptation of an Austrian headdress, became popular in all the major European armies at the start of the nineteenth century. France, as the most successful land power, was the arbiter of military fashion and adopted the shako for all her infantry in 1806. This pattern had cords round it and was replaced in 1810 by a more austere shako, as shown here. At first it was worn with a diamond-shaped plate, but then was replaced by a plate similar to the one illustrated. The 54th seem, however, to have followed a regimental fad by displaying the Emperor's head on their gilt-embossed badge, as most regiments simply had the regimental number stamped beneath the eagle. The brass chin scales are also an addition of 1812. Above the red, white and blue cockade is a red woollen ball. Company colours were displayed here and perhaps the red was once orange for the 3rd Company. The 1st wore green, the 2nd blue and the 4th violet. The 54th Regiment served almost continuously in the Peninsula. (Wallis & Wallis.)

20: British officer's shako, 56th Foot, 1812–16. When the stovepipe infantry shako adopted in 1800 was discarded, it was replaced by a black-felt shako, known as the Waterloo or, occasionally, the Belgic shako. It was about one inch wider at the bottom than the top, the top was flat and 7 inches in diameter, and the back was 6¾ inches in height. The raised front, which gave the shako its distinctive appearance, had a binding of black braid and suspended across it was a festoon of twisted or plaited cord, with tassels hanging down the right side. The cord was gold and crimson for officers, white for other ranks and green for light infantry. The plume, which was of the same colours as on the 1800 shako, and the cockade were placed on the left side. The plate, gilt for officers and brass for other ranks, was 5½ inches deep by 3¾ inches wide and displayed, beneath the crown, the 'GR' cypher and the number. More elaborate regimental versions of the plate exist. The specimen illustrated, made by Hawkes and Co., has had its cords replaced. The badge is brass gilt and it had been used to suggest that this may be a non-commissioned officer's headdress. (Wallis & Wallis.)

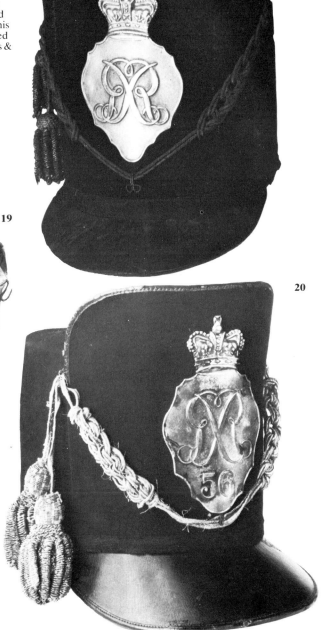

18

19

20

21

21: British officer's shako, 43rd Light Infantry, 1813. After the 1800 stovepipe shako was replaced in 1812, the Light Infantry do not seem to have adopted the new pattern on a very large scale, preferring to retain the old pattern, although now made of felt and more tapered towards the top. The example shown here has inside a label saying 'Lieut. Kershaw, 43rd Regt'. William Kershaw joined the 43rd in 1813, the regiment having covered themselves in glory in the Peninsula as part of the Light Division. The felt cap has a leather sunken top and leather peak, and a black silk turban round it. The plaited cords and the copper gilt chin scales are later features, both appearing in the Army for the first time in the 1812 uniform changes, but neither being shown by Hamilton Smith in his print of the 52nd Light Infantry. Smith does, however, show a plume, a feature missing here, although the leather cockade is present. The gilt bugle horn badge was first ordered for light infantry in 1811. (Wallis & Wallis.)

22: Prussian other rank's shako, Landwehr Infantry, c. 1815–17. The black felt shako has a black leather top and peak. A black leather band surrounds both the top and bottom and is joined on each side of the shako by a vertical black leather stripe. The chin scales are brass. The white cap lines are braided and are draped across the front of the shako, fastening at the top on each side. Lines and tassels hang from the right side. The shako plate is a black disc with a white border. In the centre of the disc is a silvered Landwehr cross. On the upper arm of the cross appears 'Mit Gott', across the arms on each side is 'Fur König und Vaterland', and on the lower arm is '1813', the year in which the Landwehr was organised. Above the shako plate is a black and white cloth field badge ('Feldzeichen'). Although the Landwehr cross as shown here is usually thought to be Prussian in origin, some military historians affirm that this type of cross, bearing the cypher of Tsar Alexander I, was used in 1812 by Russian militia 'opolchenie'). (Musée Royal de l'Armée, Brussels.)

23

24

23: United States enlisted man's shako, c. 1821–32. Showing a marked European influence, this bell-top headdress is of black leather, now badly worn. The small black leather cockade at the top front of the shako bears a brass button with a modified U.S. Arms design. The initial 'A' (for Artillery) appears on the shield on the breast of the eagle on this button. The brass eagle and shield shako plate is pierced with the number '3', indicating the 3rd Artillery Regiment. A yellow worsted cord of chain-like design is draped across the front of the head-dress. The yellow pompon at the top front of the headdress and the brass chin scales are missing from this specimen. (The Smithsonian Institution.)

24: United States infantry officer's shako, 1825. A typical bell-top shako of polished black leather, with a black leather peak or visor. The chin scales are brass. At the top front of the shako is a black leather rosette with a brass button bearing the Arms of the U.S. The shako plate is a silvered eagle with a U.S. shield on its breast. In its right talon the eagle grasps an olive branch and in its left it holds a bundle of arrows. Gold braid loops are draped from the top of each side of the shako down across the front, as well as about the back. Two gold tassels hang from the right side and a white pompon decorates the top front. (West Point Museum Collections.)

25: United States bell-top shako, c. 1829. There is some question as to whether this is a militia headdress or one worn by a cadet at the United States Military Academy at West Point. The black leather shako has a slightly domed top and a narrow black leather band around the bottom. At the top front is a black pompon in a brass holder. Below this is a small black leather rosette. The chin scales and bosses are brass. The brass shako plate is in the form of a diamond, with laurel leaves decorating the edges. In the top centre of the plate is an eagle holding an olive branch in its beak. In its right talon the eagle holds three arrows, and in the left are bolts of lightning. At the bottom quarter of the plate are three stacked muskets with fixed bayonets, a flag, a drum and a U.S. shield. (West Point Museum Collections.)

25

26: British officer's shako, probably of a Light Infantry or Rifle Militia Regiment, 1829–44. This headdress conforms to the shape of the shako worn by the infantry of the Line, as illustrated for the 76th Foot. In detail, however, it shows some of the peculiarities of the Rifle Regiments – the black lace, boss, cap line and plaited festoon. In addition, the simple plaited brass bugle badge and chin scale bosses, and the dark blue cloth body suggest Light Infantry features. · Perhaps this specimen was worn by an officer of a Militia regiment, which could afford to spurn some of the regulations. (Wallis & Wallis.)

26

27

27: Portuguese officer's bell-top shako, early nineteenth century. The shako is of black fur felt, with a black leather top and a black leather front peak edged in gilt metal. The top of the shako body is trimmed with a wide band of gold lace. The cartouche-shaped front plate displays heraldic castles and shields with a wreath behind, all under a crown. The chin chain is gilt. A gilt lion's-head boss appears on either side of the shako and at the right top. The plume or pompon at the top front of the shako is missing. (Wallis & Wallis.)

28

28: United States militia shako, c. 1830. This shako is of black leather with a flat top. A narrow brass band surrounds the top and a black leather band appears around the rear bottom half. The brass peak or visor is attached to the cap by a narrow brass band (which is itself part of the visor) and by several small brass rivets. This arrangement gives the simulated appearance of a brass chin strap. The cap plate is a brass eagle with outstretched wings with a U.S. shield on its breast. There is an olive branch in the right talon and three arrows in the left. At the top front of the cap is a small black leather rosette with a brass button bearing the design of an eagle and shield. Braided gold cord drapes from this button across the cap to attach to the left side of the peak. (West Point Museum Collections.)

29

29: Swedish infantry officer's shako, c. 1830. The black beaver body has a black leather top and black leather edging at top and bottom. The peak and chin strap are black leather. At the top front is a red wool ball pompon, and below it is a gilt scroll bearing the inscription 'Kongl Bohus Lans Reg'. This scroll is over a gold-coloured leather 'Kokarde'. At the bottom front of the shako is a gilt cartouche and crown, with the Arms of Sweden within the cartouche. (Kimball P. Vickery Collection.)

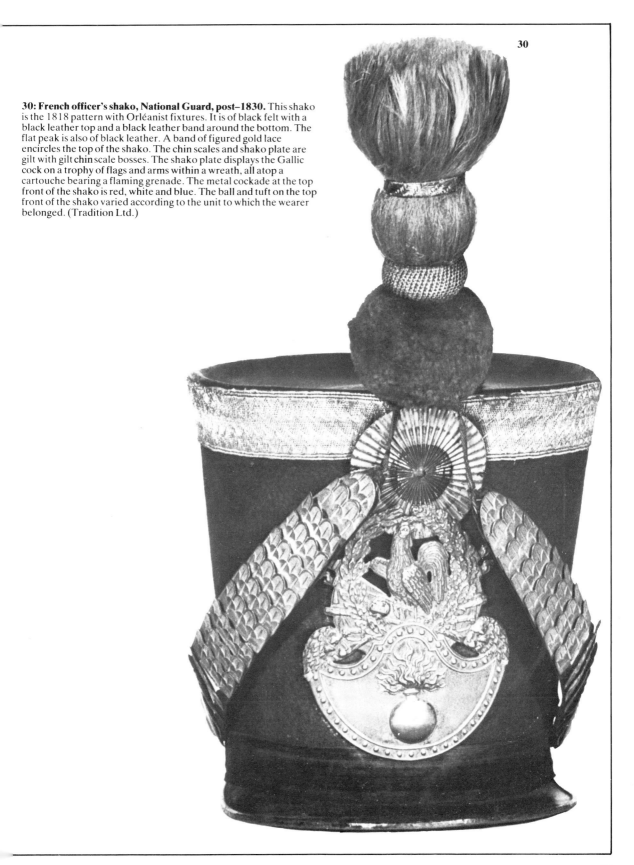

30: French officer's shako, National Guard, post–1830. This shako is the 1818 pattern with Orléanist fixtures. It is of black felt with a black leather top and a black leather band around the bottom. The flat peak is also of black leather. A band of figured gold lace encircles the top of the shako. The chin scales and shako plate are gilt with gilt chin scale bosses. The shako plate displays the Gallic cock on a trophy of flags and arms within a wreath, all atop a cartouche bearing a flaming grenade. The metal cockade at the top front of the shako is red, white and blue. The ball and tuft on the top front of the shako varied according to the unit to which the wearer belonged. (Tradition Ltd.)

31: British officer's shako, 13th Light Dragoons, 1830–41. The black velvet shako was, according to the Dress Regulations, to have a gold lace band, gilt scales and gold line. The plume was to be of white drooping cocktail feathers, but the one shown here is white horsehair, as depicted in the Mansion and Eschauzier print of the 13th. The plate, which for all the Light Dragoons took the shape of a Maltese Cross, had in the centre a laurel wreath encircling a strap on which appeared the motto 'Viret in Aeternum'; within the strap were the numerals 'XIII'. On the bases of the top and bottom arms of the cross, the Regiment bore their battle honours, 'Peninsula' and 'Waterloo'. The badge was gilt with silver panelling on the cross, and a silver centre. This bell-top shako was introduced in 1830 and replaced by a straight-sided one in 1844. A new pattern was ordered for the 13th in 1841, but this presumably conformed to the old in general appearance. (Wallis & Wallis.)

31

32

32: United States enlisted man's shako, 1832–51.
Although this headdress is referred to in the U.S. service as a cap, it is of the classic shako form, and was worn by infantry and artillery units of the Regular Establishment. This infantry specimen is of black beaver with a black leather top, chin strap and convex, unstitched peak or visor. A black leather band appears around the bottom of the shako. The adjustable chin strap has a brass buckle and is attached at each side of the headdress by plain brass buttons. The infantry device is a horn suspended from four cords tied in a three-loop bow. It is of white metal. A brass eagle, with a U.S. shield on its breast, has an olive branch in the left talon and three arrows in the right. Above the eagle is a plume-holder in the form of a flaming grenade, but the plume is missing. Artillerymen wore crossed cannons on the front of this shako.

33: French National Guard musician's shako, 1830. The black felt shako has a black leather top and peak and a black leather band around the bottom. The chin scales, bosses and shako plate are white metal. Round the top of the shako is a wide band of white braid. The shako plate displays a cock on a cartouche, bearing a Medusa head surrounded by a trophy of musical instruments. At the top front is a metal cockade in red, white and blue. The plume is also red, white and blue. (Kimball P. Vickery Collection.)

34: United States enlisted dragoon's shako, 1833–51. This French-influenced headdress is slightly conical. The top and peak visor are of black leather but the body is of black beaver. A black leather band encircles the bottom. The shako plate consists of an eight-pointed brass heraldic star, upon which is superimposed an eagle in silvered brass. Intertwined yellow cords are draped across the front and back of the shako, and a yellow tassel hangs from the left side. Yellow cap lines, terminating in 'waffles' and tassels are also attached to the left side. Above the front plate appear a plume-holder, in the form of a flaming bomb, and a white horsehair plume. (The Smithsonian Institution.)

34

35: United States beaver top hat, c. 1835–40. This is a specimen of one of the simplest forms of military headdress. It consists merely of a front plate and plume attached to an ordinary civilian black beaver top hat, worn by a member of a Burlington, Connecticut, militia unit. It is decorated at the front with a rectangular, silvered copper plate with scalloped top and bottom. There is a floral border round the plate. The centre bears an eagle, with a U.S. shield on its breast, holding an olive branch in the left talon and arrows in the right. There is an arc of thirteen stars (one for each of the thirteen original colonies) above the eagle. Between this arc of stars and the eagle appears a curved ribbon bearing the national motto 'E Pluribus Unum'. Behind the eagle there is a trophy of arms. The plume is made of red and black ostrich feathers. This hat, an example of economy, contrasts sharply with the expensive and ornate headdress of the period worn by wealthy militia units. (Guthman Collection.)

36

36: British officer's shako, 76th Foot, 1835–44. The headdress shown here is the infantry version of the bell-top shako adopted by the Light Cavalry in 1830. That for the Line was black beaver mounted on felt, with a sunken top measuring 11 inches in diameter, and leather bands round the top and bottom and down the sides. From 1829–30, this shako was worn with a swan-feather plume for officers, but the latter was replaced in 1830–35 by a red and white hackle plume. Other ranks wore an upright worsted plume until 1835, when all ranks adopted a ball, white over red for the Line, white for Grenadiers, green for Light Infantry and black for the Rifles. The regimental badge was placed on a star plate for officers, and this example shows a cut star, with the regimental number, '76', enclosed in a laurel wreath. Above is an elephant and the scroll, 'Hindoostan', to commemorate service in India; and below is the battle honour, 'Peninsula'. At first other ranks wore a similar universal pattern brass star and crown plate, but in 1839 this was replaced by a circular badge bearing the number of the regiment. (Wallis & Wallis.)

37: Swiss other rank's shako, c. 1840–50. A black felt shako with a black leather top and edging, and a flat black leather peak. The shako plate, chin scales and bosses are of white metal. The plate is in the form of a shield bearing the motto 'Liberté et Patrie' in the field. Above the shield is a metal red and white cockade. At the top front of the shako is an orange wool pompon. (Norm Hobson Collection.)

38: Russian infantry officer's shako, c. 1840–46. The obvious feature of this shako is the ridiculously long plume which at one time was worn on the military headdress of many nations. It is dark green, with a leather top and peak, and a black leather band round the bottom. A gilt crown apears above the Imperial Russian double-headed eagle, with a shield on its breast showing St. George slaying the dragon. White-plaited cords are draped across the front of the shako, and white cap lines with 'waffles' and tassels hang from the left side. The plume is a black wool. (Musée Royal de l'Armée, Brussels.)

39: Prussian officer's field cap (Feldmutz), 10th Landwehr Hussar Regiment, c. 1843–52. This unusual and interesting headdress is of black felt, with a black leather top. A narrow black leather band surrounds the cap approximately one-third of the way down from the top. A semi-circle of narrow black leather simulates the effect of a turned-up peak. The chin scales are silvered, as is the number '10' at the centre front of the cap. The field badge (Feldzeichen) and the silvered Landwehr cross appear on the left side of the cap instead of on the front. The field badge is of silvered cord with a black velvet centre. Silver cap lines with 'waffles' and acorns hang from the left side of the cap. (Musée Royal de l'Armée, Brussels.)

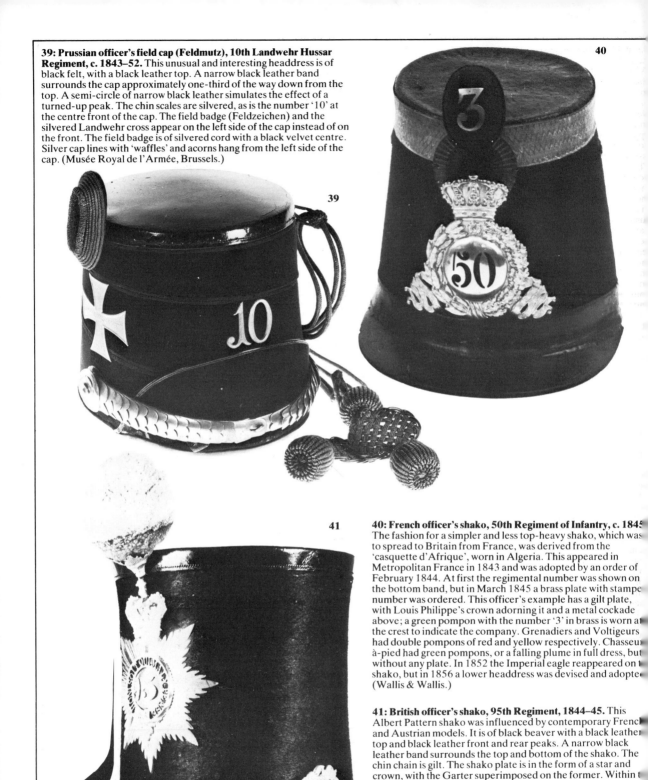

40: French officer's shako, 50th Regiment of Infantry, c. 1845. The fashion for a simpler and less top-heavy shako, which was to spread to Britain from France, was derived from the 'casquette d'Afrique', worn in Algeria. This appeared in Metropolitan France in 1843 and was adopted by an order of February 1844. At first the regimental number was shown on the bottom band, but in March 1845 a brass plate with stamped number was ordered. This officer's example has a gilt plate, with Louis Philippe's crown adorning it and a metal cockade above; a green pompon with the number '3' in brass is worn at the crest to indicate the company. Grenadiers and Voltigeurs had double pompons of red and yellow respectively. Chasseurs à-pied had green pompons, or a falling plume in full dress, but without any plate. In 1852 the Imperial eagle reappeared on the shako, but in 1856 a lower headdress was devised and adopted. (Wallis & Wallis.)

41: British officer's shako, 95th Regiment, 1844–45. This Albert Pattern shako was influenced by contemporary French and Austrian models. It is of black beaver with a black leather top and black leather front and rear peaks. A narrow black leather band surrounds the top and bottom of the shako. The chin chain is gilt. The shako plate is in the form of a star and crown, with the Garter superimposed on the former. Within the circle formed by the Garter is the number '95'. The ball tuft at the top front of the shako is red and white. (Tradition Ltd.)

42: British officer's shako, 3rd Light Dragoons, 1844–45.
When the bell-top infantry shako was replaced in 1844 by the straight-sided Albert pattern, the Light Dragoons were not long in following suit. Indeed a new pattern was approved in January 1843 but it does not seem to have been issued in many cases until 1845. The 1846 Dress Regulations describe it as black beaver, 7 inches deep at the front, 8 inches at the back, and 8 inches in diameter at the top. The sunken top, the peak and the band round the base of the headdress were all of patent leather. A gold lace band 1¾ inches wide ran round the top, and 1-inch-deep gold embroidered the peak. The gold cap lines had acorn or olive ends. The white plume was either of feathers for officers or of horsehair for other ranks and for officers in undress or serving in India. The curb chin strap ended in rose-shaped bosses, except in the case of the 3rd Light Dragoons, who displayed, in white metal, their own badge of a horse. The shako plate was continued from the previous pattern, and the one here illustrated has a gilt Maltese Cross with silver cut quarters. The gilt centre bears a silver horse and number 'III', with the motto 'Nec aspera terrent' above. The regimental title and battle honours appear in the arms of the cross. Martens's prints of the First Sikh War show the 3rd, who greatly distinguished themselves in the campaign, wearing this shako. In fact white-covered ones were often worn in India and in the Crimea, and an oilskin foul-weather version was also used. In 1855 the Light Dragoons again followed the infantry and adopted a lower shako, with a forward cant to it. (Wallis & Wallis.)

43: French infantry grenadier officer's shako, 1845–48. The black felt body has a black leather top and peak, and there is a wide band of black leather round the bottom. A broad band of ornamented silver braid encircles the top of the shako. The chin scales are silver-plated as are the bosses and the shako badge. Flaming grenades decorate the bosses. The shako badge is a globe over crossed fasces and clasped hands, surmounted by a cock with outstretched wings. On either side of the globe appears a flag bearing the inscription 'Liberté Egalité, Fraternité'. A scroll at the bottom bears the words 'République Française'. Above the badge appears a red, white and blue cockade and there is a red pompon at the top of the shako. (Kimball P. Vickery Collection.)

44: Turkish officer's shako, c. 1850. This Turkish shako, in the French style, is a most unusual collector's item. It is of red felt with a flat black peak. There is a wide band of figured gold lace round the top of the shako, as well as down the front. A gold cord extends down each side. The black leather chin strap is attached on each side by a gilt button. The shako plate consists of a gilt trophy of flags and a crescent, and at the top of the shako is a gilt star on a green cockade. Above this is a green pompon. (Norm Hobson Collection.)

45: British other rank's shako, Royal Gloucestershire Yeomanry, c. 1850. Although equipped as Light Dragoons, the shako of the Gloucestershire Yeomanry was not as tall as that of their regular counterparts, but instead followed the Austrian fashion, simply because a sister-in-law of one of the officers was married to the Austrian Ambassador. The officer's pattern was blue with wide gold lace round the top, and a tall green feather plume. The headdress illustrated was made by Hawkes, Mosley and Co. and is also of dark blue cloth. The lace is yellow cloth with red stripes, the lines and plaited cord are yellow and the cockade is yellow metal. (Wallis & Wallis.)

46: French infantry other rank's shako, 1852–55. The body, peak, edging round top and bottom, and the reinforcing stripes in the form of an inverted 'V' on each side are all black leather. The brass shako plate is in the form of an eagle standing on a grenade which is pierced with the number '19'. Behind the eagle's head is a red, white and blue metal cockade. At the top front are two pompons, yellow over black. This type of shako was particularly popular with militia units in the United States at this period. (Kimball P. Vickery Collection.)

47: United States enlisted man's artillery shako, c. 1854. This cap is slightly conical, and has a flat top. It is made of dark blue cloth and has an encircling red cloth welt which forms an inverted 'V' in front. The chin strap and the flat peak are of black leather, and the former is fitted with a brass buckle. It is secured to each side of the cap by a small brass button. The brass cap plate is in the form of the modified Arms of the U.S. The brass 'A' below the eagle indicates that the wearer belongs to Company A. The red pompon at the top front of the cap and the red cloth welt identify this as an artillery headdress. The pompon and welt varied in colour according to service – red for artillery, light blue for infantry, medium green for riflemen, yellow for engineers and crimson for ordnance. This headdress was never particularly popular with the troops. (The Smithsonian Institution.)

48: Swiss Chasseur other rank's shako, c. 1855. The black felt body has a black leather top and black leather edging around the top and bottom. The flat peak is black leather. At the top front is a black plume with a red woollen pompon below. Under the pompon is a silver and blue metal cockade with a brass button in the centre, and the two are connected by a strip bearing simulated scales. Below the cockade are crossed sharpshooters' rifles and the numeral '2'. (Kimball P. Vickery Collection.)

43

44

45

47

46

48

49

49: British officer's shako, 37th Foot, 1855–60. In January 1855, the British infantry shako was again remodelled along continental lines and given a forward tilt. The officer's pattern was of black felt, $5\frac{1}{4}$ inches deep in front but $7\frac{1}{8}$ inches deep behind, and $1\frac{1}{2}$ inches less in diameter at the top than at the bottom. The sunk top, front and back peaks, the chin strap, and the band round the base were all of black patent leather. The colours of the ball tufts were unchanged, and the Light Infantry wore a drooping green plume. The badges were gilt for officers and brass for other ranks, and followed a universal pattern of a crown above a Garter proper; the Garter was set on a rayed star, and within it appeared the number of the regiment. Fusiliers had a grenade as a badge, and Light Infantry had the bugle and strings. (Wallis & Wallis.)

50: United States enlisted man's forage cap, c. 1858–72. This is the famous French-influenced cap worn by the Union Army in the American Civil War. Of dark blue cloth, it has a black leather peak and a black chin strap with brass buckle. The brass side buttons bear the U.S. Arms. A brass initial, identifying the company to which the wearer was assigned, was authorised for wear on the front of this cap. However, during the Civil War, devices identifying the wearer's corps or branch of service were sometimes worn on the flat top of this cap. (The Smithsonian Institution.)

50

51

51: United States militia enlisted man's shako, c. 1860. At this period a number of American militia units adopted this shako which was imported directly from France. Of black leather, it has a flat top and flat black leather peak or visor, and there are narrow black leather bands round the top and bottom. Two narrow black leather stripes in the form of an inverted 'V' reinforce the sides. There is a black metal ventilator on each side near the top. At the top front is a small brass holder, supporting a red woollen ball to which a green pompon is attached. Beneath it is a stamped red, white and blue metal cockade. The brass shako plate is in the form of a wreath of oak and laurel leaves, within which is a slightly domed disc bearing a light infantry bugle-horn. On the top of the wreath is an eagle with outstretched wings with a U.S. shield on its breast. The right talon grasps an olive branch while the left holds three arrows. (West Point Museum Collections.)

52: Danish light infantry officer's shako, c. 1860. The black felt body has a black leather top and front and rear peaks. The chin scales and bosses are silver, and under the right boss is a red and silver kokarde. Beneath the white plume is a silver sunburst shako plate, with a gilt centre displaying the Arms of Denmark. (Kimball P. Vickery Collection.)

52

53

53: Swedish infantry other rank's shako, c. 1860. The black felt body has yellow edging. There is a black leather band round the bottom and a black leather peak. The yellow pompon bears the numeral '6', and the cockade is yellow leather. (Kimball P. Vickery Collection).

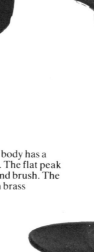

54

54: Swiss infantry other rank's shako, c. 1860. The black felt body has a black leather top and black leather edging at top and bottom. The flat peak is black leather. At the top front is a red and green pompon and brush. The cockade at the centre front is silver and green, and below it in brass appears '12R'. (Kimball P. Vickery Collection.)

55

55: British officer's shako, High Peak Rifles, 1860–69 pattern. In 1860 the infantry received a new-pattern shako in succession to that shown for the 37th Foot for 1855–60. Its forward tilt owed something to France for its inspiration, and the shako was made of dark blue cloth mounted on a cork base. The cloth was ribbed or stitched all over so that the headdress would retain its shape in wet weather, and it was duly dubbed the 'quilted' shako. Its height was 4 inches at the front and 6¾ inches at the back. Colonels and Lieutenant Colonels were distinguished by two bands of regimental lace round the top of the shako, and Majors by one. The gilt plate was mounted on an eight-pointed star with a crown above; that for other ranks was brass. The specimen shown here is rather more ornate than the simple style of the regular army, and was worn by a Derbyshire volunteer unit, the High Peak Rifles. The fittings are silvered and the band is red. (Wallis & Wallis.)

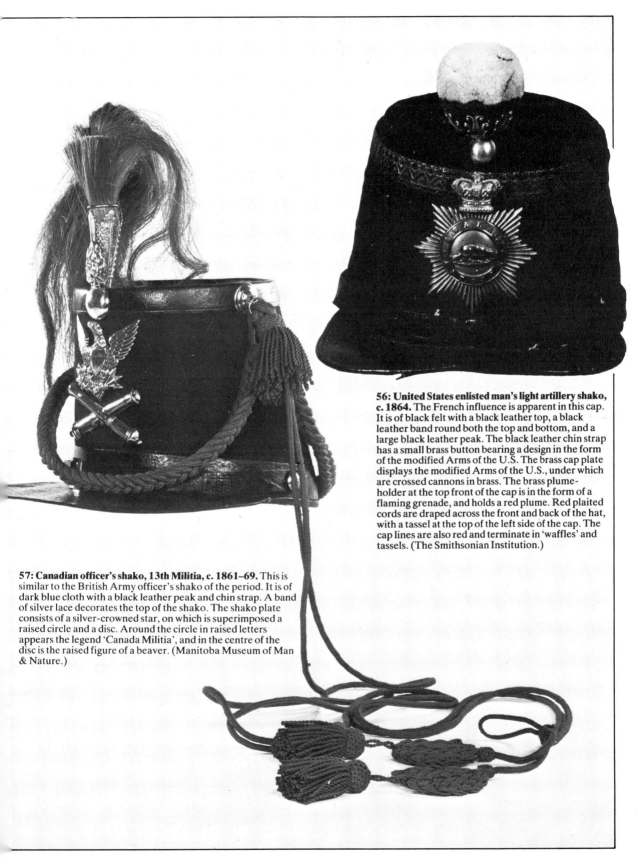

56: United States enlisted man's light artillery shako, c. 1864. The French influence is apparent in this cap. It is of black felt with a black leather top, a black leather band round both the top and bottom, and a large black leather peak. The black leather chin strap has a small brass button bearing a design in the form of the modified Arms of the U.S. The brass cap plate displays the modified Arms of the U.S., under which are crossed cannons in brass. The brass plume-holder at the top front of the cap is in the form of a flaming grenade, and holds a red plume. Red plaited cords are draped across the front and back of the hat, with a tassel at the top of the left side of the cap. The cap lines are also red and terminate in 'waffles' and tassels. (The Smithsonian Institution.)

57: Canadian officer's shako, 13th Militia, c. 1861–69. This is similar to the British Army officer's shako of the period. It is of dark blue cloth with a black leather peak and chin strap. A band of silver lace decorates the top of the shako. The shako plate consists of a silver-crowned star, on which is superimposed a raised circle and a disc. Around the circle in raised letters appears the legend 'Canada Militia', and in the centre of the disc is the raised figure of a beaver. (Manitoba Museum of Man & Nature.)

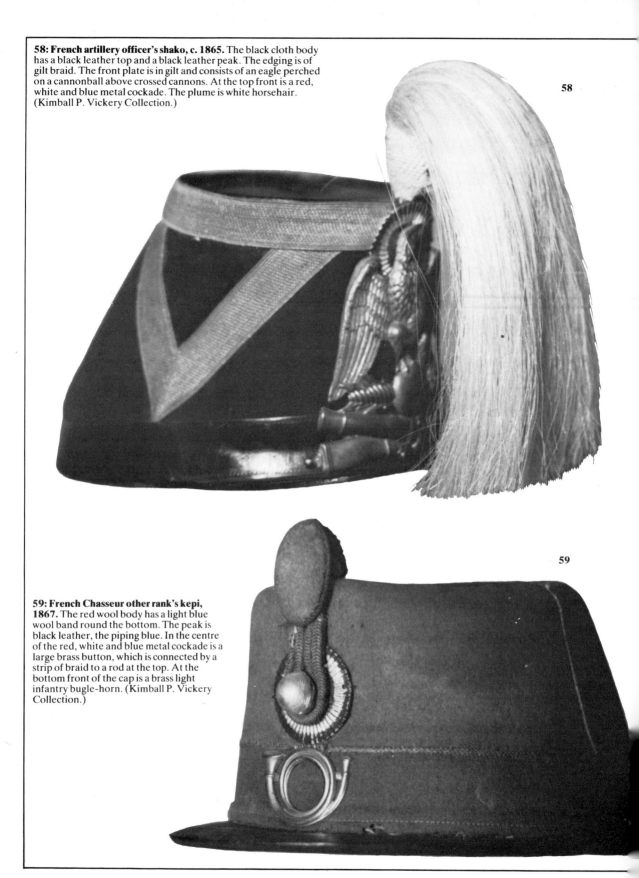

58: French artillery officer's shako, c. 1865. The black cloth body has a black leather top and a black leather peak. The edging is of gilt braid. The front plate is in gilt and consists of an eagle perched on a cannonball above crossed cannons. At the top front is a red, white and blue metal cockade. The plume is white horsehair. (Kimball P. Vickery Collection.)

58

59

59: French Chasseur other rank's kepi, 1867. The red wool body has a light blue wool band round the bottom. The peak is black leather, the piping blue. In the centre of the red, white and blue metal cockade is a large brass button, which is connected by a strip of braid to a rod at the top. At the bottom front of the cap is a brass light infantry bugle-horn. (Kimball P. Vickery Collection.)

60: British officer's shako, 13th Lancashire Rifle Volunteers pattern of 1869–78. This shako, of the pattern worn by the regular infantry between 1869 and 1878 has a dark blue body, and its flat black leather peak is furbished with a silvered chin chain and bosses. Two rows of narrow silver braid go round the top of the shako, with a single stripe of silver braid down each side. The silvered shako plate consists of a heraldic star and crown. Superimposed on the star is a rimmed circle on which appears 'Lancashire Rifle Volunteers', and within which is a rose over the number '13'. A blue pompon is supported in a floral-type holder bearing the 'VR' (Victoria Regina) cypher. (Wallis & Wallis.)

61: British officer's shako, 12th Regiment of Foot, pattern of 1869–78. The last-pattern shako to be worn in the British Army followed its predecessor in its French appearance and in being made of dark blue cloth mounted on cork. It was introduced by order of June 1869 and worn by all infantry regiments until 1878 and by their depot companies until 1881. It measured 4 inches high in front, and 6½ inches at the back, while the slightly sunken crown was 6 inches long by 5½ inches across. Round the top were two strands of gold braid, one quarter of an inch wide and one-quarter of an inch apart, but colonels and Lieutenant Colonels had two lines of half-inch lace. Braid was also placed up the sides and back, and round the bottom. The peak was flat and made of black patent leather. The chin strap, when not worn down, could be hooked to a lion's head at the back. All the metal fittings were gilt, and the ball holder bore a 'VR' cypher. The ball itself was red and white. The plate measured 3 inches by 3¾ inches deep, and normally displayed the regimental number within the Garter bearing the motto 'Honi Soit Qui Mal y Pense'. However, that shown here (the 12th Foot) had the castle and key of Gibraltar in the centre, with scrolls bearing the motto 'Montis Insignia Calpe' below and the honour 'Gibraltar' above. It was in silver, but the laurel wreath and crown were gilt. (Wallis & Wallis.)

62: Swiss infantry officer's shako, c. 1870. The black beaver body has a black leather top and edging, and black leather front and rear peaks. There are three rows of gold lace round the bottom. At the top front is a red and white ball pompon. Under this is a silver and black metal cockade over crossed rifles and the numeral '4', both of which are in gilt metal. (Kimball P. Vickery Collection.)

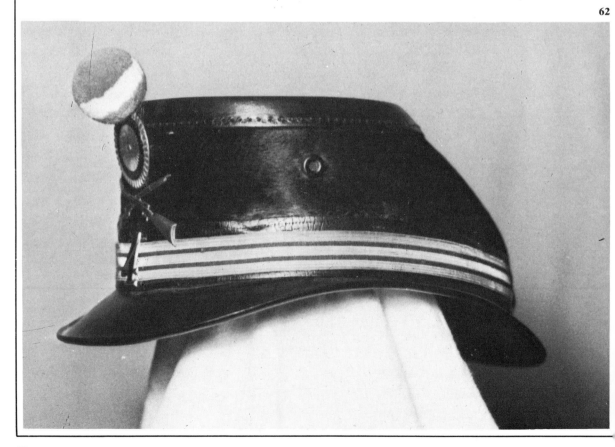

63: Netherlands infantry officer's kepi, c. 1870. This has a black wool body with a black leather chin strap and peak. The gilt side button bears the design of a light infantry bugle-horn. Red piping decorates the top half of the kepi, and there are two lines of widely spaced gold braid around the bottom. At the front is a gilt badge in the form of a light infantry bugle-horn. (Kimball P. Vickery Collection.)

64: Russian artillery other rank's kepi, c. 1870. The black felt body has a black leather edging round the top and bottom, and a black leather top. The flat peak is also of black leather. On the front appears the double-headed Russian eagle with a silver, orange and black cockade. Above the eagle is a scroll bearing the regimental battle honours in Russian. A black hair plume decorates the top front of the kepi. (Kimball P. Vickery Collection.)

65: United States artillery kepi, 1872. Another French-influenced
United States Army headdress is this Model 1872 artillery cap. It is of
dark blue cloth with a flat black unstitched peak and black leather chin
strap. The brass side buttons bear the U.S. Arms. The braid around the
top and bottom and down the sides of the cap is red, as is the pompon.
A black metal ventilator is in the centre of the top of the cap. The
insignia on the front consists of a modified version of the U.S. Arms,
under which appear the crossed cannons of the Field Artillery, all of
yellow metal. The cap insignia varied according to the arm, as did the
colour of the braid. (The Smithsonian Institution.)

66: United States enlisted man's kepi, c. 1872. This is the Model 1872
forage cap with the Model 1875 infantry insignia (crossed rifles). It is
yet another modification of the French kepi, of dark blue cloth, with a
flat black leather peak. This peak is unstitched along the front and side
edges. The black leather chin strap is held on each side of the cap by a
small brass button bearing the U.S. Arms. The brass cap insignia
identifies the cap as belonging to a member of Company A, 25th U.S.
Infantry. (The Smithsonian Institution.)

65

66

67: French Hussar shako, 1874 pattern. This sky-blue felt shako, with its polished black leather peak, has a silvered chin chain, peak edging and bosses. A wide band of figured silver lace surrounds the top of the shako. A red, white and blue metal cockade supports a white plume. The front of the shako is decorated with silver braid knots. (Norm Hobson Collection.)

67

68

70

68: Argentinian infantry officer's kepi, c. 1880. The dark blue wool body has a black leather peak and chin strap. Four lines of gold braid encircle the middle section of the kepi, which is also decorated on the front, back and sides by three vertical lines of gold braid. The top is decorated with a gold braid quatrefoil. At the centre front of the kepi appears a blue, white and blue beaded cockade. (Kimball P. Vickery Collection.)

70: Swedish field artillery officer's shako, c. 1880. The black wool body is trimmed round the bottom with a black leather band. The top of the shako is also of black leather, as are the front and rear peaks. The top is decorated with two rows of gold braid, the lower row forming a large 'V' on each side of the shako. Within this 'V' is a sky-blue triangle. The gilt cap badge is in the form of a star with the Royal Crown and the Order of the Seraphim. In the centre appear three gilt crowns on a blue-enamelled background (the Arms of Sweden). (Kimball P. Vickery Collection.)

69: French Hussar officer's shako, c. 1890. This light blue cloth shako has a black leather band round the bottom and a black leather peak. The silvered chin chain fastens onto lion's-mask bosses and there is a silver lace band around the top of the shako. Under the silver cord ball pompon at the top front is a short strip of silver braid, a silver button and a red, white and blue cockade. At the lower front is a silvered flaming grenade. (Kimball P. Vickery Collection.)

71: Netherlands artillery officer's shako, c. 1880. The black wool body has a black leather top, peak and edging round the top and bottom. The chin chain, lion's-mask bosses and plume-holder are gilt, the latter having a black plume. The orange cockade at the top front is furnished with a gilt button. At the lower front are gilt crossed cannons with the Royal Crown. (Kimball P. Vickery Collection.)

72

73

72: Belgian rifle volunteer other rank's shako, c. 1890. This grey felt body has a black leather top and peak. There is a band of green cloth round the top and a band of black leather round the bottom. The ball pompon at the top front is green and is connected by green cord with a dull metal button in the centre of a red, yellow and blue cockade. Under the cockade are crossed rifles in dull metal. (Kimball P. Vickery Collection.)

73: Belgian Chasseur a Cheval officer's shako, c. 1890. The dark green felt body with its black leather top has a black leather band round the bottom and a black leather peak. There is a wide band of gold lace around the top. The cockade bears a gilt button displaying a light infantry bugle-horn and the numeral '2'. The plume is of dark purple feathers. (Kimball P. Vickery Collection.)

75

74

74: Prussian other rank's shako, Guard's Rifle Battalion, post–1897. The shako is of polished black leather, including the front and rear peaks, and has a straight front and a rounded back. There is no trim round the peaks. The black leather chin strap has grey-metal fittings. The grey-metal shako plate is closely patterned after the Star of the Order of the Black Eagle, and interwined in its rays is a ribbon bearing the motto 'Mitt Gott Fur König und Vaterland'. The field badge is black and white. The right-hand Kokarde is black, white and red (Imperial Germany) and the one on the left is black and white (Prussia). (Norm Flayderman Collection.)

75: Swedish Hussar officer's shako or kepi, c. 1900. The black wool body has a black leather top and black leather edging around the top and bottom. The peak is also black leather. At the top two strands of narrow gold braid intertwined with black encircle the crown. Under this braid are two rows of gold lace. At the top front is a gilt wire plume-holder with a black feather plume. The gilt shako plate is in the form of a sunburst bearing the Arms of Sweden with a blue enamelled centre. (Kimball P. Vickery Collection.)

76: British other rank's shako, Highland Light Infantry, c. 1900. Around the bottom of the dark blue cloth shako, with its flat black leather peak, is a diced band of white, red and dark green. The white-metal shako plate is in the form of the Order of the Thistle, upon which is superimposed a light infantry bugle with the monogram 'HLI' in yellow metal. Below this is an elephant and a scroll with the battle honour 'Assaye'. Above the shako plate is a corded button. At the top front of the headdress is a green ball pompon. Black cap lines, plaited in sections, fall from each side of the top of the shako across the front, and form a knot and acorns hanging from the right side. (Wallis & Wallis.)

77

77: Italian infantry (Grenadier) officer's service kepi, c. 1900. The black wool body is adorned with a black leather chin strap and peak, and a black velvet band around the bottom. There are three stripes of silver braid about the centre section and a strand of vertical red braid on each side. The silver badge in the form of a flaming grenade bears the numeral '3', to denote the number of the regiment. (Kimball P. Vickery Collection.)

78: Guatemalan infantry officer's kepi, c. 1900. The grey wool body, with its black leather peak, has a gold-lace chin strap fastened to each side by a small gilt button. The front is decorated with a gold braid knot with, in the centre, a gilt button bearing the Arms of Guatemala. (Kimball P. Vickery Collection.)

78

79: British other rank's shako, Highland Light Infantry, c. 1902. This shako was introduced in 1862. It is of dark blue cloth and has a flat black leather peak. Round the bottom of the shako is a wide band, diced white, red and dark green. A black-metal ventilator appears on each side of the shako. At the top front is a black wool corded boss with a white-metal thistle in the centre, and above it is a dark green pompon. The regimental badge appears below the corded boss and is the Star of the Order of the Thistle upon which is a light infantry bugle-horn. In the twist of the horn is the monogram 'HLI'. Above the horn is a crown, and below is an elephant, superscribed 'Assaye', on a scroll. This badge is in white metal. The black cap lines, which are plaited where they fall down across the front, encircle the shako and hang down on the right side, terminating in acorns. The black leather chin strap is missing from this specimen. (Kimball P. Vickery Collection.)

79

80: Russian officer's shako (Kiva), c. 1910. This handsome headdress, much more ornate than those worn by other nations in recent times, is of blue-green cloth with red piping. The fittings, edging and cords are silver. The brush at the top front of the shako is of silver wire. The shako plate is the Russian double-headed eagle. (Tradition Ltd.)

80

81: Swiss other rank's infantry shako, c. 1910. The black wool body has black leather top and bottom edging and black leather front and rear peaks. There is a red and white ball pompon at the top front over a red and white metal cockade bearing a white cross. Beneath this are brass crossed rifles and the brass numeral '8'. (Kimball P. Vickery Collection.)

81

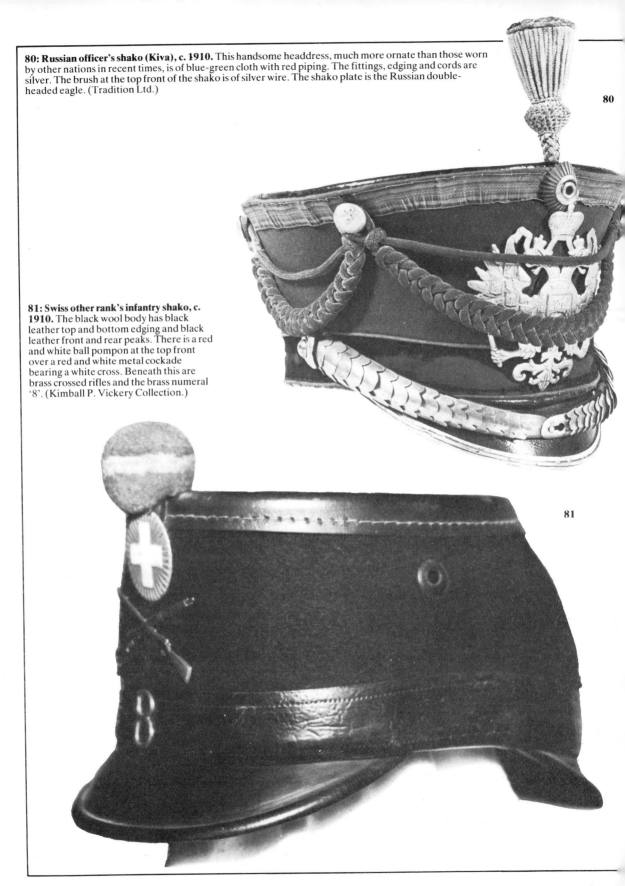

82

82: Argentinian mounted rifles other rank's shako, c. 1910.
The black wool body, with its black leather peak, has a black
leather band round the bottom. The chin scales, bosses and
edge to the peak are all brass. Interwoven pink cords droop
across the front of the shako and pink tassels hang from the
left side. A band of yellow cloth encircles the top of this
headdress. Below the red pompon at the top is a yellow
braid and brass button decoration. Underneath is a blue and
white metal cockade over the Arms of Argentina. (Kimball
P. Vickery Collection.)

**83: Prussian other rank's shako, c.
1914.** This greenish-grey felt 'Jager'
shako has a brass plate and fittings.
The chin strap is black leather. The
shako plate is in the form of the
Prussian heraldic eagle with motto. A
cloth white and black field badge
appears at the top front of the shako, a
black, white and red metal Kokarde on
the right side, and a black and white
Kokarde on the left. The felt shako
seldom appears on the collector's
market. (Norm Hobson Collection.)

83

3. Leather helmets

84: United States militia dragoon helmet, c. 1780–1810. The so-called jockey cap type of helmet known in Britain as the Tarleton helmet, is an early form of military headdress. This is an American example, with a hard black leather skull and a flat front peak or visor. It is decorated front-to-back with a strip of bearskin (which is now very much worn). A wide painted red band decorates the bottom of the skull. The painted red and black leather cockade on the left side of the skull bears a small plain brass button. Similar helmets were won by British and European armies of the period. (West Point Museum Collections.)

85

86

87

85: Bavarian Rumford universal helmet, c. 1789. This rare item of military headdress is made of thick black leather, with a black horse-hair crest. The brass helmet plate shows the Royal Arms within a floral wreath motif and with a lion's mask above it. This helmet has a wide flat front peak and a smaller flat rear peak. (Tradition Ltd.)

86: British officer's helmet, 20th Light Dragoons, c. 1796. The helmet shown is of leather and was worn by the 20th who were raised in 1791 for service in Jamaica and who wore the alligator emblem to commemorate the fact. It has a silver-plated copper crest with a red and white hair plume. The turban ends in a bun at the rear and has chains on it. While most of the regiment had the alligator and 'XXLD', as illustrated, on their badges, the trumpeters displayed a trumpet in place of the alligator and the farriers had a crossed hammer and pincers within a horseshoe. The fur-crested leather helmet worn by the British Light Cavalry proved objectionable in hot climates and in 1796 metal helmets were proposed as an alternative and adopted by at least the 8th, 20th and 25th Light Dragoons. Therefore, from c. 1797 to 1802, when the regiment returned to England, the 20th seems to have worn a helmet similar to the one illustrated, but of tin. (Wallis & Wallis.)

87: Austrian other rank's helmet, c. 1798. Reminiscent in some ways of an ancient Roman gladiator's helmet is this helmet, introduced in 1798 for almost all Austrian units. It is of thick black leather with brass fittings and hinging. The front peak is trimmed with brass but the rear one is not. The large front plate bears 'F II' (Friedrich II). The chin strap is of black leather with a brass buckle. The ornamented bosses are also brass. (Tradition Ltd.)

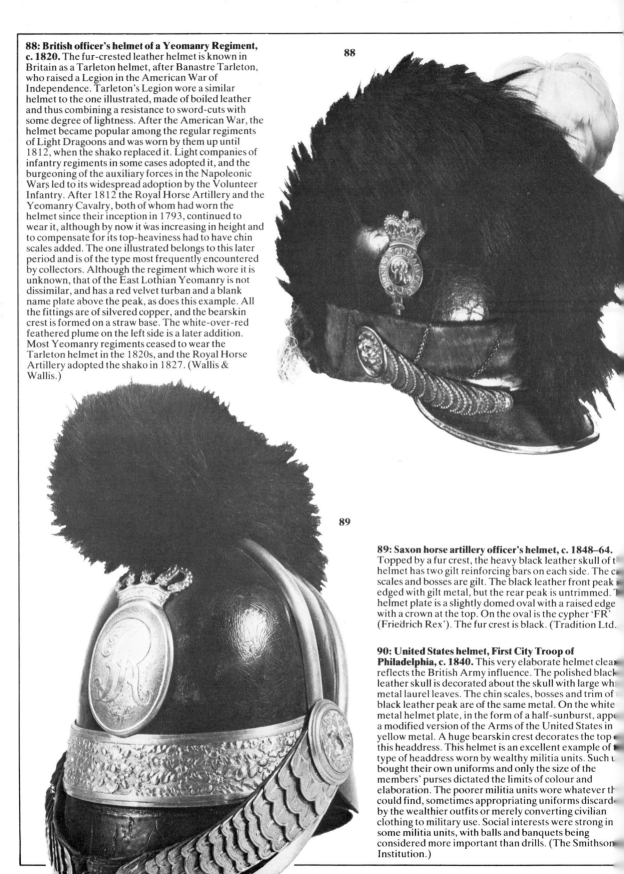

88: British officer's helmet of a Yeomanry Regiment, c. 1820. The fur-crested leather helmet is known in Britain as a Tarleton helmet, after Banastre Tarleton, who raised a Legion in the American War of Independence. Tarleton's Legion wore a similar helmet to the one illustrated, made of boiled leather and thus combining a resistance to sword-cuts with some degree of lightness. After the American War, the helmet became popular among the regular regiments of Light Dragoons and was worn by them up until 1812, when the shako replaced it. Light companies of infantry regiments in some cases adopted it, and the burgeoning of the auxiliary forces in the Napoleonic Wars led to its widespread adoption by the Volunteer Infantry. After 1812 the Royal Horse Artillery and the Yeomanry Cavalry, both of whom had worn the helmet since their inception in 1793, continued to wear it, although by now it was increasing in height and to compensate for its top-heaviness had to have chin scales added. The one illustrated belongs to this later period and is of the type most frequently encountered by collectors. Although the regiment which wore it is unknown, that of the East Lothian Yeomanry is not dissimilar, and has a red velvet turban and a blank name plate above the peak, as does this example. All the fittings are of silvered copper, and the bearskin crest is formed on a straw base. The white-over-red feathered plume on the left side is a later addition. Most Yeomanry regiments ceased to wear the Tarleton helmet in the 1820s, and the Royal Horse Artillery adopted the shako in 1827. (Wallis & Wallis.)

89: Saxon horse artillery officer's helmet, c. 1848–64. Topped by a fur crest, the heavy black leather skull of t[...] helmet has two gilt reinforcing bars on each side. The c[...] scales and bosses are gilt. The black leather front peak [...] edged with gilt metal, but the rear peak is untrimmed. [...] helmet plate is a slightly domed oval with a raised edge [...] with a crown at the top. On the oval is the cypher 'FR' (Friedrich Rex'). The fur crest is black. (Tradition Ltd.[...]

90: United States helmet, First City Troop of Philadelphia, c. 1840. This very elaborate helmet clea[...] reflects the British Army influence. The polished black leather skull is decorated about the skull with large wh[...] metal laurel leaves. The chin scales, bosses and trim of [...] black leather peak are of the same metal. On the white metal helmet plate, in the form of a half-sunburst, app[...] a modified version of the Arms of the United States in yellow metal. A huge bearskin crest decorates the top [...] this headdress. This helmet is an excellent example of t[...] type of headdress worn by wealthy militia units. Such u[...] bought their own uniforms and only the size of the members' purses dictated the limits of colour and elaboration. The poorer militia units wore whatever th[...] could find, sometimes appropriating uniforms discarde[...] by the wealthier outfits or merely converting civilian clothing to military use. Social interests were strong in some militia units, with balls and banquets being considered more important than drills. (The Smithson[...] Institution.)

91: British officer's helmet, Worcestershire Yeomanry, c. 1850. An excellent example of yeomanry headdress is this black leather helmet, introduced in 1850. The slotted brass crest is trimmed in silver and the gilt helmet plate backed with silver. The plate itself has the Royal Cypher within an oval inscribed 'Queen's Own Regiment', with the Royal Crest and supporters. Under the oval appears a ribbon bearing the legend 'Worcestershire Yeomanry'. There is a silver band around the base of the skull, silver binding to the front and rear peaks and silver chin scales attached to silver lion's-mask bosses. The red and white horsehair plume is topped with a gilt rose. (Tradition Ltd.)

92: Swiss other rank's infantry helmet, c. 1850–90. The fittings and chin scales are brass. A black fur chenille adorns the top of the headdress. There is a band of brass around the base of the skull and a brass reinforcing bar down each side. A metal rosette appears on the left side. The chin scales and bosses are of brass. The bosses bear an infantry bugle design. The rimmed oval helmet plate of brass bears the Swiss cross in silver. (Norm Hobson Collection.)

93: Swedish other rank's helmet, Life Guard Dragoons, c. 1859. This is a black leather helmet with front and rear peaks. The crest, front plate, chin scales and bosses are all of brass. On the large brass front plate appear the embossed Arms of Sweden with the Collar of the Order of the Seraphim. (Kimball P. Vickery Collection.)

94: Saxon other rank's reserve cavalry helmet, c. 1860. The helmet is of heavy black leather with brass fittings and a black wool chenille. The brass heraldic star bears a Landwehr cross, upon which are superimposed the Arms of Saxony. Both front and rear peaks are trimmed with brass edging, as is the comb. Brass strips decorate the sides of the skull, forming an inverted 'V' on each side. The heavy chin scales are also of brass. (Norm Hobson Collection.)

95: British yeomanry officer's helmet, Fife Mounted Rifles, 1860–96. This black leather helmet has plain front and rear peaks. The helmet plate consists of the silver figure of a mounted knight (The Thane of Fife) superimposed upon a gilt St. Andrew's cross, which in turn is superimposed upon a four-pointed silver star. On the lower part of the star appears the Roman numeral 'IX', and at the bottom is a silver scroll with 'FMR' in the centre. On one side of the scroll are the words 'Pro Aris', and on the other 'et Focis'. A silver plume-holder supports a white horsehair plume. (Kimball P. Vickery Collection.)

96: British officer's helmet, 1st Oxfordshire Light Horse Volunteers, 1864–70. Illustrated here is another variation of the black helmet favoured by some yeomanry, light horse volunteer and mounted rifle regiments. This particular one was worn by the Oxfordshire Light Horse, who were raised in 1864 and disbanded in 1870. The dark blue felt helmet has a black leather peak bound with white metal. All the fittings, including the comb with its ventilation holes, are of white metal. The red horsehair mane is original but it has been suggested that the red brush at the front of the crest is a later addition. The badge displays the monogram 'LOH' reversed and interlaced, with the number 'I' and crown above, and the motto 'Fortis est Veritas' below. (Wallis & Wallis.)

97: Bavarian Chevau-Légers (Dragoon) officer's helmet, c. 1870. This Bavarian 'Raupenhelm' of the Franco-Prussian War period is an interesting collector's item. The skull is polished black leather. The front and rear peaks are edged with gilt. There is a black wool comb. The black leather chin strap with its gilt lion's-head bosses has gilt buckle and end pieces. On the front of the helmet is the gilt crowned cypher 'L' (Ludwig). On the left side of the skull is a blue and silver Kokarde (Bavaria) with a plume-socket but the plume is missing. Introduced in 1800, the raupenhelm underwent several changes and modifications during its existence. (Wallis & Wallis.)

98: Luxembourg cavalry officer's helmet, c. 1900. The metal skull and peaks are covered in blue wool. The gilt lion crest and edging to the peaks are in gilt, as are the metal chin strap and the bosses with their decorative floral design. The chin strap simulates scales. A red, white and blue cockade appears just below the front of the crest. Below this cockade is a gilt badge consisting of a grenade within a wreath, with crossed lances with flags. The gilt plume-holder on the left side holds a red feather plume. (Kimball P. Vickery Collection.)

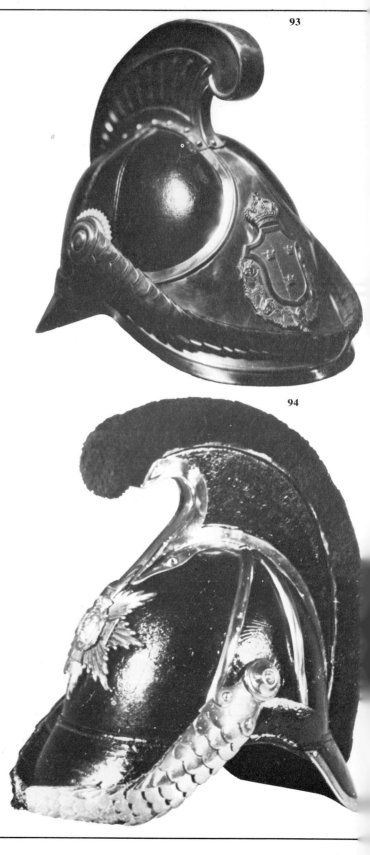

93

94

99: French Cuirassier's helmet, pre-1830. The skull and peaks are silver-coppered. The high copper-gilt comb decorated with volutes and floral leaves has mounted on it a large thick horsehair crest. An extremely ornate helmet plate covers the front of skull and extends around the bottom. In front the plate bears an oval shield upon which is the Royalist fleur-de-lis. The front and rear peaks are edged with copper-gilt. The leather-lined metal chin strap simulates chin scales and is of copper-gilt. So too are the large sunburst bosses, bearing fleur-de-lis, on either side of the skull. The side plume is missing but the holder is clear in the illustration. (Norm Flayderman Collection.)

100: French officer's helmet, Sapeurs-Pompier, c. 1822–30. In France, the fire brigade formed, and indeed continues to form, part of the Army. As such it did not fall behind in the vogue for classical-style helmets, although even in a brass parade helmet, such as this, the peak can be moved up, clear of the face. The crossed fire-axes on the peak are a clear indication of the identity of the wearer. The fleur-de-lis on the shield are Bourbon features and date the helmet to the Restoration, although it has in fact been adapted from a First Empire helmet. A black hair chenille adorns the brass crest, and a red plume embellishes the side. (Wallis & Wallis.)

100

101: French Cuirassier's helmet, post-1830. In 1821 the French dragoons and cuirassiers adopted a helmet as illustrated, but it does not appear to have been worn until about 1825 and then continued in use till 1840. The absence of a fleur-de-lis on this specimen suggests a post-1830 date. That for the dragoons was of brass, while the cuirassiers had one of steel with a brass badge. The black horsehair brush, crest and mane are offset by an upright red brush plume at the front tip of the crest. On the left is a brass plume-holder, the plume itself being missing. In 1826 squadrons were identified by the colour of a ball placed at the base of the plume – blue for the 1st squadron, crimson for the 2nd, green for the 3rd, sky-blue for the 4th, rose for the 5th, and yellow for the 6th. (Wallis & Wallis.)

102: British officer's helmet, 1st (Royal) Dragoons, 1834–43.
The fabulous Romanesque helmet illustrated here was made
entirely of gilt for officers and of brass for other ranks. The details
are well shown in the photograph (although the chin scales are
missing), but it is interesting to note that although worn during
Victoria's reign, no specimen has been discovered that bears her
arms rather than the Hanoverian ones. The regimental title was
borne on a band round the top of the peak, and the wearing of this
pattern was confined to the Dragoon Guards, and the 1st and 6th
Dragoons. The only other heavy cavalry regiment, the 2nd
Dragoons, continued, as they had done since 1807, to wear their
bearskin grenadier cap. The helmet is also found with a large
black bearskin crest stretching from front to back. This was
attached by removing the lion's head on the front of the comb,
and was worn on full dress occasions. Trumpeters and bandsmen
often wore crests of different colours, red being particularly
popular. In 1843, a new helmet was adopted, similar in shape, if
somewhat squatter, but with a long horsehair mane flowing from
the crest, and with a brush in front. (Wallis & Wallis.)

**103: British officer's helmet, 1st King's Dragoon Guards, c.
1840.** The skull and peaks are gilt, and the former is richly
ornamented along the top and down the back with a floral motif.
The helmet plate is a large half-sunburst upon which the Royal
Arms are superimposed. The regimental title appears in raised
letters on a band under the helmet plate. The gilt chin scales are
attached to each side of the skull by a rose-shaped boss. The
ornate lion crest may be removed and a large bearskin crest
substituted for dress. (Norm Hobson Collection.)

102

103

105: Belgian other rank's helmet, 1843. Among the more
handsome and sought-after metal helmets are those of the
Belgian Army. This specimen was worn by other ranks of a
Kingdom of Belgium cuirassier regiment. The skull is of white
metal with a brass comb. A silver grenade decorates the front of
the comb which is embossed with volutes and a laurel wreath
motif. A black horsehair tuft in a decorated brass holder appears
at the top front of the comb. A red feather dress plume is inserted
in a socket on the left side of the skull and a black horsehair tail
hangs from the rear of the comb. The brass chin strap of
embossed scales is attached to each side of the skull by a large
sunburst rosette, upon which is superimposed a bursting grenade.
The helmet plate, in brass, is a lion's head (the lion being the
heraldic animal in the Arms of Belgium). This helmet closely
resembles that worn by French cuirassiers of the period. (Wallis
& Wallis.)

**106: British officer's helmet, 3rd Dragoon Guards, pattern of
1847–71.** The pattern of helmet adopted for Heavy Cavalry in
1847 followed the Prussian lines already aped by the Household
Cavalry since 1843, and was known as the Albert helmet. This for
the officers was in gilt, while the other rank's was brass, and the
plume for all regiments was at first black. The issue of helmets
was in many cases delayed by up to two or three years after 1847
and in 1848 a white-metal helmet was approved for the 1st, and
later the 6th, Dragoons. The 1855 Dress Regulations give black
and red plumes for the 3rd Dragoon Guards, but the specimen
illustrated here has a white and red plume. (Wallis & Wallis.)

104: French Cuirassier's helmet, post-1840. The skull is steel with a black fur turban. The brass comb is decorated on the sides with volutes and laurel leaves, and on the front bears the head of Medusa, above a flaming grenade. At the top front of the comb is a red horsehair brush in a brass holder. A black horsehair tail hangs from the rear of the comb. In a socket on the left side of the skull is a red plume. The brass chin chains are attached to large brass bosses. (Norm Hobson Collection.)

104

106

107: French dragoon officer's helmet, 1852–70. An interesting French metal helmet is this dragoon officer's helmet of the Second Empire. The copper-gilt skull has a leopard-skin turban. The high copper gilt comb is profusely decorated with volutes and floral leaves, and the front bears a flaming grenade, above which is the face of Medusa. The front top of the comb bears a short black tuft in a copper gilt holder. A long black horsehair tail issues from the rear of the comb. On the left of the skull is a copper-gilt plume-holder. The copper-gilt chin chain is attached to each side of the skull by large copper-gilt bosses bearing a leaf motif. (Wallis & Wallis.)

108: Bavarian other rank's Cuirassier's helmet, c. 1860s. The skull is polished steel and the peaks are trimmed with brass. The brass front plate bears the initial 'L' (Ludwig). The brass chin scales are attached to a brass lion's mask on each side of the skull. A white and blue Kokarde (Bavaria) appears above the lion's mask on the left of the skull. A black horsehair chenille decorates the brass comb. (Norm Hobson Collection.)

109: British Guards officer's helmet, 1871 pattern. Among the more sought-after helmets are those of the British Dragoons Guards Regiments. Here is a fine example of the last (1871) pattern of a helmet of an officer of the 3rd (Prince of Wales)

Dragoon Guards. The helmet is gilt with a gilt chin chain and bosses. The horsehair plume is black and red. The helmet plate of silver, gilt and enamel bears the Garter superimposed on a cut star. The plume, coronet and motto of the Prince of Wales occupies the centre of the helmet plate. (Wallis & Wallis.)

110: British trooper's helmet, 1st West Yorkshire Yeomanry Cavalry, post-1876. In 1876 the 1st West Yorkshire Yeomanry adopted a white-metal helmet, and by 1878, if not earlier, this had a white plume. The mounts on the helmet followed in pattern those adopted for Regular Heavy Cavalry in 1847 and were silver-plated for officers. The officer's badge had a plated rose on a gilt centre, and a gilt garter and scroll, bearing the title of the regiment, on a plated cut star. These gilt fittings were brass for other ranks. In 1889 the regiment became the Yorkshire Dragoons, but the spike plume-holder had already replaced the acanthus one at an earlier date. (Wallis & Wallis.)

111: United States mounted unit helmet, State of Georgia Militia, c. 1880. The German and British influence is evident in this white-metal helmet with gilt fittings and a yellow plume. The side buttons bear crossed sabres. The brass half-sunburst front plate bears the Georgia State Seal in brass. This consists essentially of three columns supporting an arch inscribed with the word 'Constitution', upon which an eagle is perched with outspread wings. Around the columns is entwined a ribbon bearing the words 'Wisdom Justice Moderation'. (The Smithsonian Institution.)

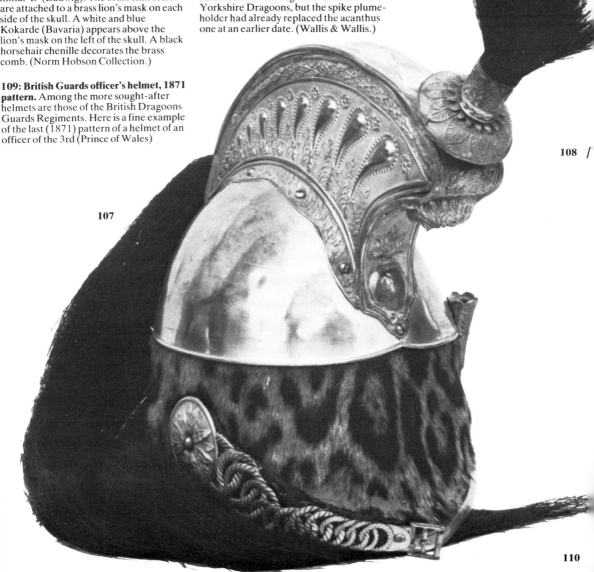

108

107

110

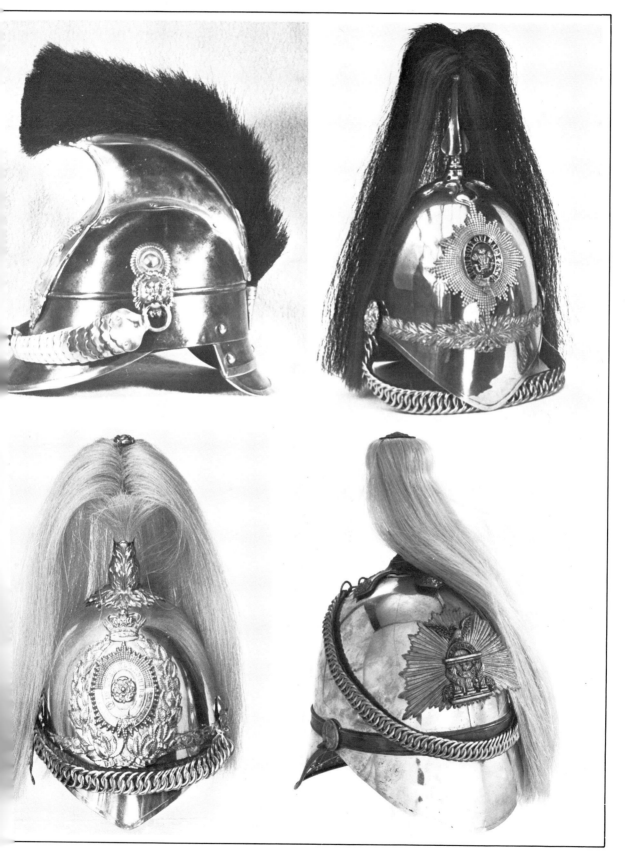

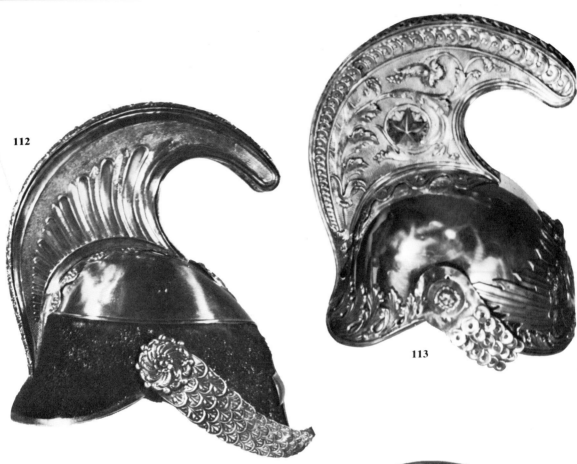

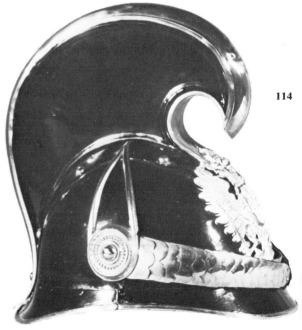

112: Italian (Royal Piedmont) cavalry officer's helmet, c. 1900.
This is an unusual and decorative specimen. The polished steel skull is decorated with a distinctive high gilt comb. The bottom half of the skull and the front and rear peaks are covered with black fur. The highly decorated chin scales and bosses are gilt. A silver cross, with arms of equal length, appears as a helmet plate. (Norm Hobson Collection.)

113: Spanish cavalry officer's helmet, c. 1900. This ornate helmet has a polished steel skull with gilt fittings and edging. The Spanish Arms, in silver, appear on the gilt helmet plate which is in the form of a half-sunburst. The high gilt comb, decorated in a floral motif, has a silver star on each side. Around the bottom of the skull is a wide gilt floral decorative band. Part of the gilt chin scales are missing. The chin scale bosses are also gilt. (Norm Hobson Collection.)

114: Austrian dragoon helmet, 1905 pattern. Among some of the more ornate helmets are those of the Austrian dragoons of pre-World War One days. This is a 1905 pattern helmet (privately purchased) of black lacquered metal for a warrant officer or a sergeant major. Issue helmets are of black leather, for warrant officers and below. The high black comb is trimmed in tombak (yellow metal). Tombak pieces form an inverted 'V' on each side of the skull, and there are tombak chin scales, bosses and edging to the front and rear peaks. The tombak helmet plate is in the form of the crowned double-headed eagle with the Arms of Austria on its breast. (Norm Hobson Collection.)

115: German other rank's gala helmet, Saxon Garde-Reiter-Regiment, post-1907. The history of this heavy cavalry regiment dates back to 1683. However, this particular lion-crested helmet – one of the most beautiful and sought-after collector's items – was worn only from 1907 until World War One, and only a very few of them were ever made. The skull, peak and lobster-tail back are of tombak. The edging of the peak, of the lobster-tail back and around the base of the skull is in white metal, as is the lion crest. The lion stands with his forepaws on a shield, upon which, within a polished oval, appear the crowned initials 'FAR' (Friedrich Augustus Rex). The chin scales are tombak. The helmet plate is a heraldic star in white metal with the Arms of Saxony in tombak. (Tradition Ltd.)

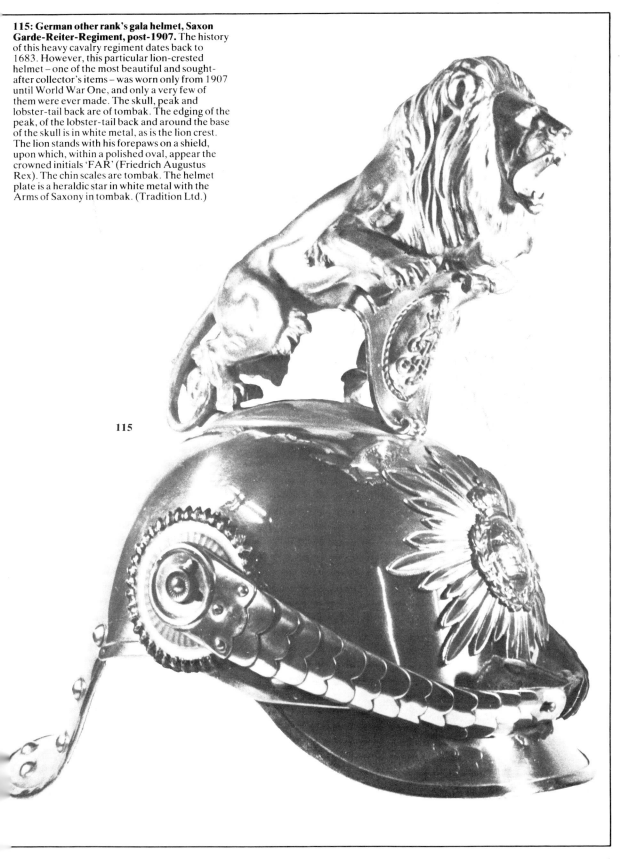

115

116: French Chasseur helmet, c. 1910. This helmet has a steel skull, a steel front peak and a short lobster-tail back edged in brass. The brass comb is lavishly decorated and has a black horsehair tail at the rear. The front of the comb bears the head of Medusa. The chin scales and decorated bosses are of brass, as is the plume-socket on the left side of the skull. The brass helmet plate bears a silver star, from which radiate silver rays. (Wallis & Wallis.)

117: French Chasseur a Cheval helmet, c. 1910. This headdress is like the French chasseur helmet of the same period (Plate 209), except for the helmet plate. In this case the brass helmet plate bears a silver light infantry bugle-horn with silver rays radiating from the horn. (Wallis & Wallis.)

118: Prussian other rank's Cuirassier helmet, c. 1914. The all-steel skull has a plain round front peak and lobster-tail back. The fittings, edging and helmet plate are grey metal. The plate is in the form of the Prussian heraldic line eagle. Earlier Prussian other rank's curassier helmets were somewhat more elaborate, with brass chin scales, edging and helmet plate. The spike was also more graceful in form. This specimen has a leather chin strap and the usual Kokarden, i.e., black, white and red (Imperial Germany) on the right, and black and white (Prussia) on the left. (Norm Flayderman Collection.)

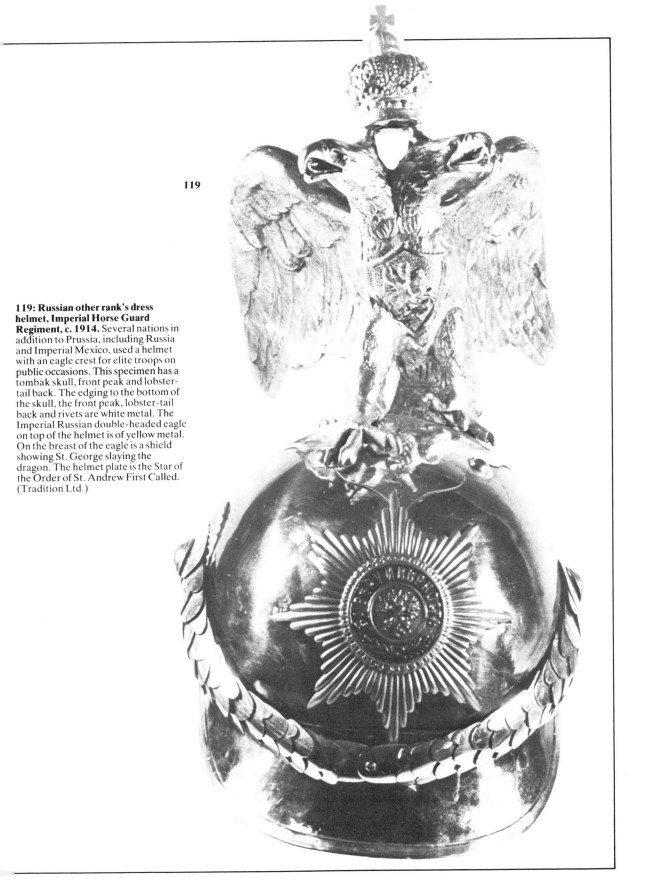

119: Russian other rank's dress helmet, Imperial Horse Guard Regiment, c. 1914. Several nations in addition to Prussia, including Russia and Imperial Mexico, used a helmet with an eagle crest for elite troops on public occasions. This specimen has a tombak skull, front peak and lobster-tail back. The edging to the bottom of the skull, the front peak, lobster-tail back and rivets are white metal. The Imperial Russian double-headed eagle on top of the helmet is of yellow metal. On the breast of the eagle is a shield showing St. George slaying the dragon. The helmet plate is the Star of the Order of St. Andrew First Called. (Tradition Ltd.)

5. Pickelhauben and spiked helmets

120: Prussian infantry officer's Pickelhaube, 1842. The reign of the Prussian Pickelhaube began with this pattern of 1842. It was copied by the majority of other armies, including the British Army and the United States Army. Of heavy black leather, it has a high skull and deep square cut peaks. This specimen is an infantry officer's model. The spike, cross-type spike base, helmet plate, chin scales and front peak edging are all in gilt. The well-detailed helmet plate is in the form of the Prussian heraldic eagle with the initials 'FR' (Friedrich Wilhelm Rex) on its breast. It differs slightly from the later-model Prussian line eagle and does not have the motto 'Mit Gott Fur König und Vaterland'. On the right side of the skull, under the chin scale boss, is a metal Kokarde in black and white, the colours of Prussia. The Pickelhaube underwent several changes during succeeding years. The skull became lower in 1857, 1860, 1867, 1871, 1887 and 1890. After 1857 square-cut peaks were retained only for general officers, Landwehr officers, and for certain elite units, including dragoons and palace guards, and in the Bavarian service. A round peak was used by other units. The metal edging around the front peak and the chin scales were abandoned in 1887 but were reinstated four years later. Still later the chin scales were replaced by leather chin straps on other ranks' helmets. (Musée Royal de l'Armée, Brussels.)

121: Russian other rank's helmet, Imperial 95th Infantry Regiment, mid-nineteenth century. Some units of the Imperial Russian Army wore a Pickelhaube similar to that worn by Prussian soldiers. In lieu of the spike, an ornament in the form of a flaming bomb was worn. This other rank's helmet is of heavy black leather with brass fittings. The crowned double-headed Imperial Eagle has a shield upon its breast showing St. George slaying a dragon. The eagle is above a cartouche bearing the cut-out numerals '95'. The peaks have no metal trim. It is worth noting that the crowned double-headed Imperial Russian Eagle is of Byzantine origin. As early as the 1490s this particular form of eagle had been adopted by Tsar Ivan III to reinforce his claims that he was a legitimate successor to the Byzantine emperors. The double-headed Byzantine eagle remained the official crest of Russia from that time until 1917 when the Imperial reign ended. (Norm Hobson Collection.)

121

122

122: Prussian grenadier officer's Pickelhaube, 1842. This spiked helmet is similar to the one illustrated in Plate 65, except that instead of the line eagle it has the grenadier eagle, namely the Prussian heraldic eagle with an oval shield on its breast bearing the cypher 'FWR' (Friedrich Wilhelm Rex). (Norm Hobson Collection.)

73

123: Baden artillery other rank's helmet, c. 1849. The heavy black leather skull has a brass edging and fittings. The front plate is of brass and represents the crowned Baden griffin standing upright on a floral wreath and supporting a shield bearing the initial 'L' (Grand Duke Leopold). This helmet is similar to the Prussian other rank's artillery Pickelhaube introduced in 1846, with a ball ornament instead of the spike to symbolise the spherical cannonball of the era. In the Prussian service the support of the ball was longer and somewhat more decorative. (Norm Hobson Collection.)

123

124

124: Hanover other rank's helmet, 1849–58. In 1849 Hanover, then an independent kingdom, adopted the Prussian Pickelhaube. It was worn until 1858. Shown here is an early model other rank's helmet. Of heavy black leather, it has a brass spike, spike base, chin scales and edging. The helmet plate, in white metal, is the traditional white horse of Hanover. One red and white (silver) Kokarde is worn, on the right side. The early model Prussian-type helmets, particularly those of the smaller Kingdoms and States, are extremely rare. (Norm Flayderman Collection.)

125: Swedish other rank's helmet, c. 1850. This Swedish version of the 1842 Prussian Pickelhaube has a brass spike, spike base, peak edging and helmet plate. The plate is in the form of the Arms of Sweden surrounded by the Collar of the Order of the Seraphim. (Wallis & Wallis.)

125

126

126: Parma other rank's helmet, Grenadier of the Guards, 1851. This black leather Pickelhaube, another example of Prussian influence, is, except for the helmet plate and part of the edging, similar to the Prussian Model of 1842. The helmet plate, chin scale bosses and spike base bear the Bourbon lilies or fleur-de-lis. Parma was a short-lived Duchy, later incorporated into the Kingdom of Sardinia and then into the Kingdom of Italy. (Tradition Ltd.)

**127: British officer's helmet, Royal Marines Light Infantry,
1878.** At one time the British Royal Marines also wore a
Prussian-influenced helmet, as shown by this Home Service
1878-pattern specimen. The cork helmet is covered with blue
cloth and has gilt-metal fittings and edging. The helmet plate is
in the form of the Royal Marines badge, a laurel wreath around
a strap and buckle, all superimposed upon a star, at the top of
which is a crown. The strap bears the Royal Marines motto 'Per
Mare Per Terram', within which is a silver globe showing the
eastern hemisphere. Above the strap is a ribbon bearing the
word 'Gibraltar'. Under the wreath appears an upright anchor
and below it is a light infantry bugle. (Wallis & Wallis.)

127

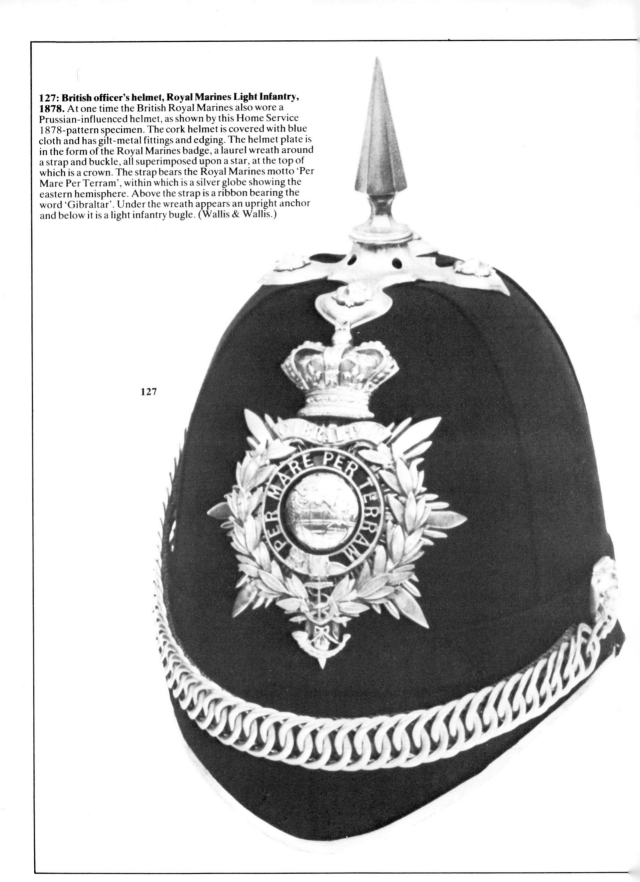

128: Canadian officer's helmet, 26th Middlesex Light Infantry, c. 1880. The Prussian influence in Canada is shown in this British Home Service 1878-pattern helmet, which is made of cork, covered with dark green cloth. The fittings and edging are white metal. The helmet plate is an eight-pointed star with a crown above, and, within a laurel wreath, a strap with a buckle, bearing the legend 'Middlesex Light Infantry – Defence Not Defiance'. In the centre of the plate appears the numeral '26'. (Manitoba Museum of Man & Nature.)

128

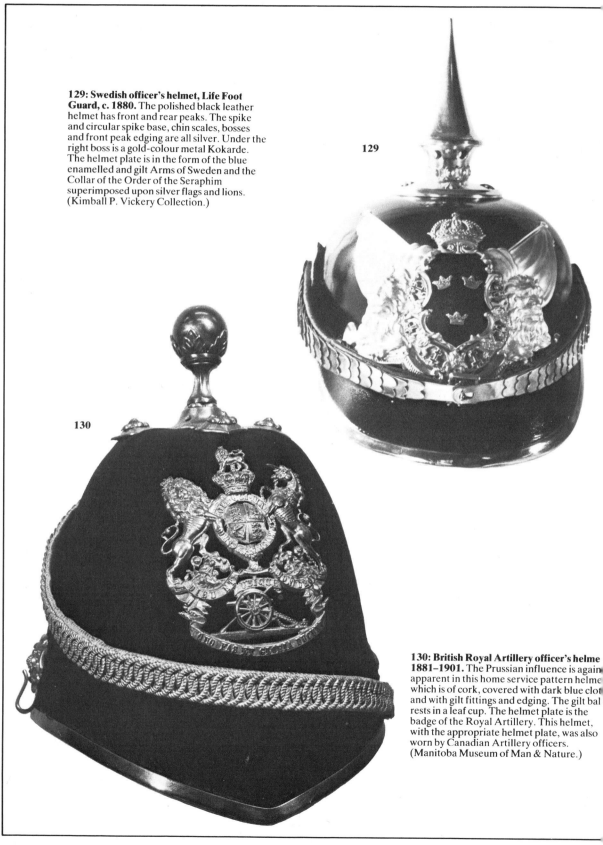

129: Swedish officer's helmet, Life Foot Guard, c. 1880. The polished black leather helmet has front and rear peaks. The spike and circular spike base, chin scales, bosses and front peak edging are all silver. Under the right boss is a gold-colour metal Kokarde. The helmet plate is in the form of the blue enamelled and gilt Arms of Sweden and the Collar of the Order of the Seraphim superimposed upon silver flags and lions. (Kimball P. Vickery Collection.)

129

130

130: British Royal Artillery officer's helmet 1881–1901. The Prussian influence is again apparent in this home service pattern helmet which is of cork, covered with dark blue cloth and with gilt fittings and edging. The gilt ball rests in a leaf cup. The helmet plate is the badge of the Royal Artillery. This helmet, with the appropriate helmet plate, was also worn by Canadian Artillery officers. (Manitoba Museum of Man & Nature.)

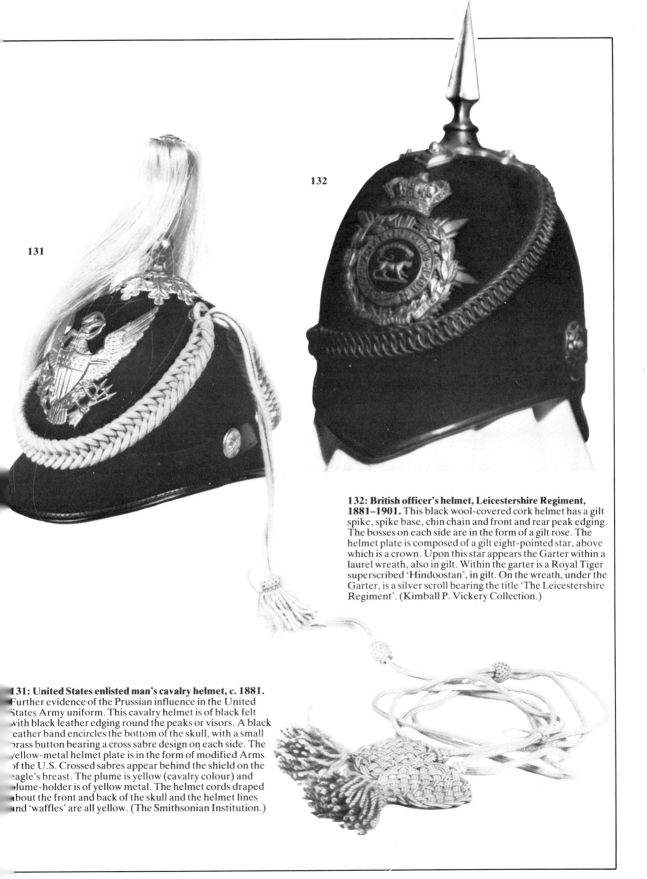

132: British officer's helmet, Leicestershire Regiment, 1881–1901. This black wool-covered cork helmet has a gilt spike, spike base, chin chain and front and rear peak edging. The bosses on each side are in the form of a gilt rose. The helmet plate is composed of a gilt eight-pointed star, above which is a crown. Upon this star appears the Garter within a laurel wreath, also in gilt. Within the garter is a Royal Tiger superscribed 'Hindoostan', in gilt. On the wreath, under the Garter, is a silver scroll bearing the title 'The Leicestershire Regiment'. (Kimball P. Vickery Collection.)

131: United States enlisted man's cavalry helmet, c. 1881. Further evidence of the Prussian influence in the United States Army uniform. This cavalry helmet is of black felt with black leather edging round the peaks or visors. A black leather band encircles the bottom of the skull, with a small brass button bearing a cross sabre design on each side. The yellow-metal helmet plate is in the form of modified Arms of the U.S. Crossed sabres appear behind the shield on the eagle's breast. The plume is yellow (cavalry colour) and plume-holder is of yellow metal. The helmet cords draped about the front and back of the skull and the helmet lines and 'waffles' are all yellow. (The Smithsonian Institution.)

133

133: Mexican officer's Pickelhaube, c. 1890. This helmet has a gala plume in lieu of the spike. Skull and peaks are polished black leather. The front peak edging is gilt, as is the plume-holder supporting a black plume. The gilt chin scales have a red, silver and green cockade on each side. The gilt helmet plate is in the form of a Mexican eagle, perched on cactus, holding a snake in its beak (the Arms of Mexico). On one side of the eagle appears the initial 'B' and the other 'Z'. Both are in silver. (Kimball P. Vickery Collection.)

134

134: Netherlands other rank's dress helmet, Royal Marine Corps, post-1896. The German-influenced spiked helmet, introduced in 1896, is somewhat similar to the modified Pickelhaube used in the British, Canadian and United States Armies. This cork helmet is covered with dark blue cloth. The spike and spike base, chin chain, helmet plate and side buttons are of yellow metal. The highly detailed helmet plate is in the form of the Corps badge, a star with a floral wreath and crossed anchors, and in the centre a strap and buckle, the strap bearing the motto 'Je Maintiendrai'. Within the circle formed by the strap is the Netherlands lion on a blue-enamelled background. The side buttons bear an upright anchor. The above specimen is of the type currently worn. These helmets are the gift of the citizens of Rotterdam where the Corps headquarters is now located. (The Royal Netherlands Marine Corps.)

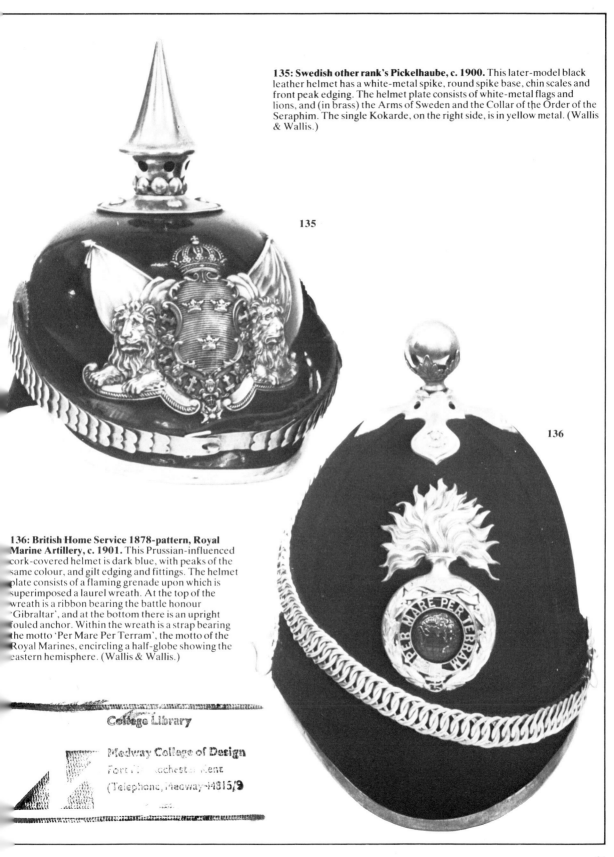

135: Swedish other rank's Pickelhaube, c. 1900. This later-model black leather helmet has a white-metal spike, round spike base, chin scales and front peak edging. The helmet plate consists of white-metal flags and lions, and (in brass) the Arms of Sweden and the Collar of the Order of the Seraphim. The single Kokarde, on the right side, is in yellow metal. (Wallis & Wallis.)

135

136

136: British Home Service 1878-pattern, Royal Marine Artillery, c. 1901. This Prussian-influenced cork-covered helmet is dark blue, with peaks of the same colour, and gilt edging and fittings. The helmet plate consists of a flaming grenade upon which is superimposed a laurel wreath. At the top of the wreath is a ribbon bearing the battle honour 'Gibraltar', and at the bottom there is an upright fouled anchor. Within the wreath is a strap bearing the motto 'Per Mare Per Terram', the motto of the Royal Marines, encircling a half-globe showing the eastern hemisphere. (Wallis & Wallis.)

137: British officer's Home Service Helmet, Cheshire Regiment, post-1901. The Prussian influence is again strongly marked in this cork helmet, covered with dark blue cloth. All the metal fittings and edging are in high-quality gilt. The bosses on the sides of the skull are in the form of roses, chin chain fastens to a hook at the rear of the spike base. The helmet plate is a star with a crown at the top. On the star is the Garter within which, on a black velvet background, appears a small star and circle. In the circle are the plume and coronet of the Prince of Wales. Under the Garter there is a ribbon bearing the legend 'The Cheshire Regiment'. (Wallis & Wallis.)

137

138

138: German officer's Pickelhaube, Queen Olga's Dragoons (1st Württemburg) No. 25, early 1900s. This pickelhaube provides additional evidence of the wide variety of Imperial German helmet plates to be collected. The square front peak, which is common to dragoon regiments, and the cross-shaped spike base are of special interest. The helmet plate, chin scales, edging and fittings are all in gilt. The helmet plate is in the form of the Arms of Württemburg. The right Kokarde is black, white and red (Imperial Germany), while that on the left is black and red (Württemburg). An interesting variation on this dragoon helmet plate occurs in the case of the King's Dragoons (2nd Württemburg), No. 26, which has the Star of the Order of Württemburg superimposed on the shield of the Württemburg Arms. (Wallis & Wallis.)

139: Baden infantry officer's helmet, early 1900s. This is the final form of the famed Pickelhaube, with a lower and more rounded skull. The skull and peaks are of polished black leather, and the front peak is rounded. The gilt spike, edging, fittings and helmet plate are all of very high quality. The helmet plate is in the form of the Arms of Baden, a griffin supporting the shield of Baden. Under the griffin and shield appears a ribbon bearing the motto 'Mit Gott F. Fuerst U. Vaterland'. The right Kokarde is black, white and red (Imperial Germany), while the left one is gold (yellow) and red (Baden). Before the formation of Imperial Germany only one Kokarde was worn, on the right side, in the colours of the state (Land), but after the formation of Imperial Germany, the Imperial Kokarde was worn on the right side and the State Kokarde on the left. Helmet plates differed according to the Land and might differ even within the state. In the case of Prussia there was a wide variety of helmet plates according to certain regiments and services. (Wallis & Wallis.)

140: Mexican officer's Pickelbaube, post-1905. This Prussian-influenced Pickelhaube is almost identical in form with the Imperial German spiked helmet of the time. The helmet is of polished black leather with a gilt spike, spike base, helmet plate, chin scales and peak edging. The plate is in the form of the Mexican eagle standing on cactus leaves and grasping a snake in its beak. The cockades on each side of the helmet are coloured silver, orange and green. For parade (gala) a plume was worn in lieu of the spike. For general officers this was a white feather plume. Staff and field grade officers had a black feather plume on, while those of junior officers were in black horsehair. Cadets wore a white horsehair plume. Other ranks did not wear a Prussian-type uniform. The Prussian-influenced uniform was worn for only a comparatively short time, from 1905 to 1914. (Norm Hobson Collection.)

141: German other rank's artillery helmet, Mecklenburg Field Artillery, c. 1910. This is typical of the final version of the Imperial German artillery helmet. It is of black leather, with brass edging and fittings. The helmet plate is in the form of the Arms of Mecklenburg-Strelitz. Helmets such as this, from the smaller German states, are fairly rare. (Wallis & Wallis.)

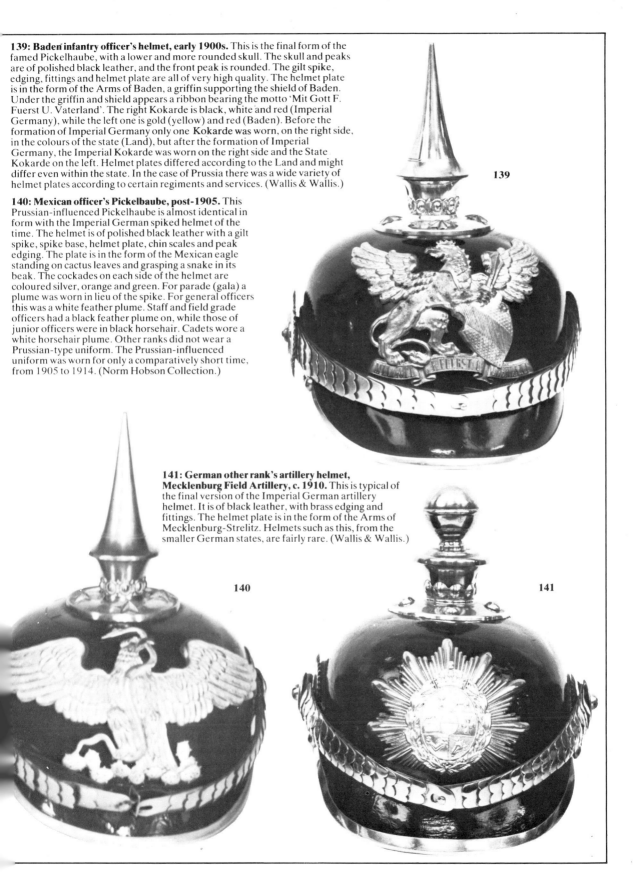

139

140

141

142: German officer's Pickelhaube with white plume, 1st Baden Life Guard Grenadiers (No. 109), c. 1914. This is a black leather helmet with gilt fittings and edging. Superimposed on the front plate, which is the griffin and shield of Baden, is the star and cross of the Order of Fidelity or Loyalty. This is an example of the wide variety of helmet plates which occurred in the Imperial Germany Army. (Tradition Ltd.)

142

143: German bandmaster's helmet, 78th Field Artillery Regiment (8th Saxon), c. 1912. In some instances in the Imperial German Army a plume was substituted for the spike on the Pickelhaube for dress (gala). This bandmaster's black leather helmet has a rounded peak edging in brass. The chin scales and the plume spike are also brass. The white-metal and brass helmet plate is an eight-pointed star bearing the Arms of Saxony. The right-hand Kokarde is black, white and red (Imperial Germany), and the left one is white and green (Saxony). The plume is red. Other than general officers, who wore plumes of varying colours according to their State (Land), and musicians, who wore red, officers and other ranks wore either white or black plumes according to the organisation to which they belonged. (Wallis & Wallis.)

143

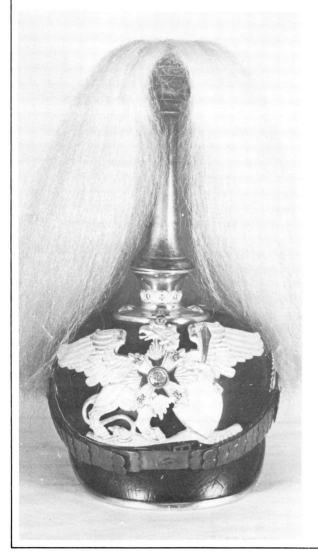

144: Prussian other rank's Pickelhaube, c. 1914. A greenish-grey hard felt Pickelhaube with grey-metal fittings, including spike, helmet plate and peak edging. The Prussian heraldic eagle helmet plate has the motto 'Mitt Gott Fur Koenig und Vaterland', and on the eagle's breast are the letters 'FR', (Friedrich Rex). The chin strap is of reinforced khaki cloth. The right Kokarde is black, white and red (Imperial Germany), while the left one is black and white (Prussia). These felt helmets were worn by a number of German States (Lander), with the appropriate helmet plate and Kokarde. (Norm Hobson Collection.)

145: Russian Guard Cuirassier Pickelhaube, c. 1914. The tombak skull has a round front peak and lobster-tail back, all being encircled by white-metal edging. The gilt-brass spike is in the form of a grenade with an elongated flame. The front plate, in the form of the Star of the Order of St Andrew First Calied, has a white-metal eight-pointed heraldic star, in the centre of which is a silver-rimmed blue-enamelled band bearing in gilt letters the legend in Russian, which translated reads 'For Faith and Loyalty'. Within the circle on a gilt-brass background is a black-enamelled double-headed Imperial Russian eagle with a small St. Andrew's cross in gilt-brass on its breast. This helmet is a very rare collector's item. (Tradition Ltd.)

146: Prussian officer's grenadier cap (Grenadiermutze), 32nd Grenadier Regiment, c. 1760.
Typical of the grenadier caps of that era, this mitre-type cap, particularly early examples of it, is very rare today. The above museum specimen has a gilt front plate decorated with trophies of arms and the so-called eagle of Frederick the Great, with a crown and the motto 'Pro Gloria et Patria'. The cap is of dark green cloth, trimmed with gold braid. The top of the cap terminates in a gilt half-grenade with flame. The wide band surrounding the bottom of the cap is decorated on the sides and back with a gilt Prussian eagle above a trophy of arms and flags. (Musée Royal de l'Armée, Brussels.

146

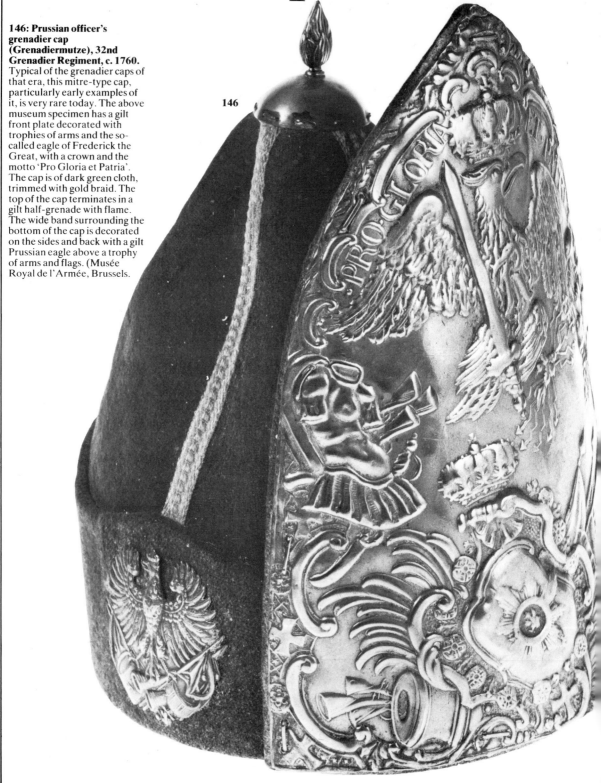

147: British officer's mitre cap, Grenadier Company 43rd Foot, c. 1740–9. The front of this headdress is buff velvet edged with gold; below the gold crown, with its crimson velvet cap and silver jewels, is the foliate 'GR' cypher, also in gold. The intertwined thistles and roses on either side are in gold, but the centre of the rose is crimson and the flower of the thistle silver. The back of the cap is scarlet, and the turn-up at the bottom, bearing the grenade and the number '43', buff velvet; all the lace and embroidery is gold, with the exception of the sword-blades which are silver. The cap is 11½ inches high, excluding the tassel at the top, which is a later addition. The embroidered Grenadier cap was a British peculiarity and this example can probably be attributed to the regiment that was later renumbered the 42nd and subsequently became the Black Watch. (Wallis & Wallis.)

147

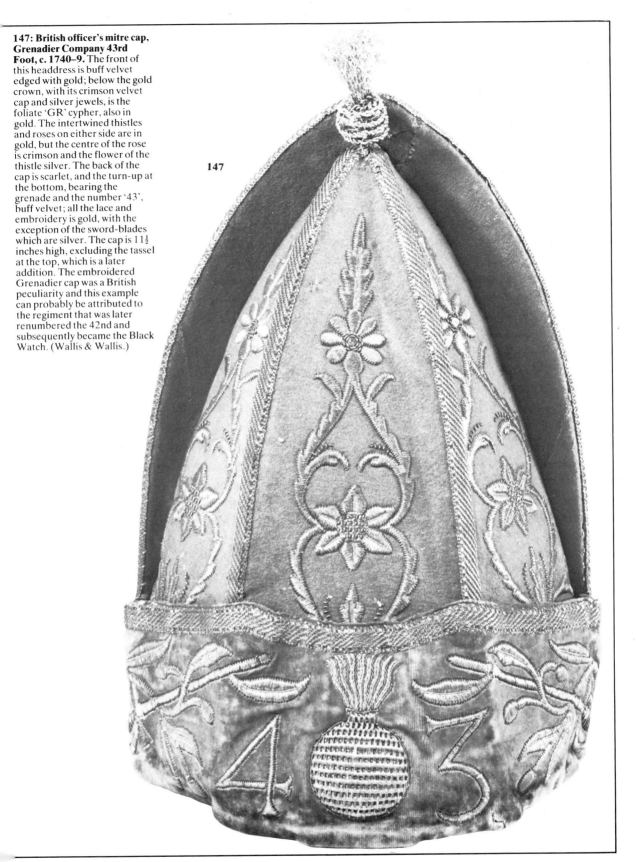

148: British officer's Racoon-skin cap, Royal Fusiliers, c. 1890. The chin chain is gilt and the regimental badge is the Garter, ensigned with a crown on the ball of the grenade, is in gilt and enamel. Within the Garter is a rose, the Garter in blue enamel with gilt letters and the rose in white and red. (Wallis & Wallis.)

149: Austrian other rank's grenadier cap, c. 1830. This interesting black bearskin cap has a large brass front plate bearing the crowned double-headed Austrian eagle. At each end of the plate is a flaming grenade. (Kimball P. Vickery Collection.)

149

150: Prussian other rank's grenadier cap (front view), 1st Foot Guards, 1894 pattern. The white-metal, mitre-shaped front plate is elaborately decorated with grenades and trophies of arms. At the top of the plate is a large crown. In the centre is the eagle of Frederick the Great. A ribbon above the eagle bears the motto 'Semper Talis' About the base of the cloth portion of the cap is a wide white-metal band, decorated on the sides of the cap with a grenade and on the rear with a grenade and trophies. The cloth part of the cap is red, with three lines of white tape. The red and white pompon worn at the apex of the front plate is missing from this specimen. The chin scales are of white metal and were added in 1896. The above cap was worn by the 1st and 2nd Battalions. The fusiliers of this regiment wore a similar cap, except that the cloth cap was yellow with white tape, trim, the pompon had a yellow central band, and the ribbon above the eagle bore the legend 'Pro Gloria et Patria'. Grenadier caps of this regiment and also of the Kaiser Alexander Guard Grenadier Regiment No. 1 occasionally appear on the collectors' market and command a very high price. (Norm Hobson Collection.)

151

151: Prussian other rank's grenadier cap (side view), 1st Foot Guard, 1894 pattern. This side view of the cap illustrated in Plate 150 shows the elaborate metal band about the bottom of the cap, as well as the red cloth cap trimmed with white tape. The 1st Guard Regiment of Foot was the most elite regiment in the Imperial Germany Army. Sometimes known as 'The First Regiment in Christendom', it traced its origin back to one of the regiments in the Great Elector's army in the 1600s. Prussian princes were enrolled in the regiment as lieutenants when ten years old. (Norm Hobson Collection.)

7. The mirleton and busby

152: Prussian Flugelmutze, von Ruesch or 'Black' Hussar Regiment, c. 1750s. This high conical cap with long loose wing was known in Germany as a Flugelmutze or a Schackelhue and in France as a mirleton. The long cloth wing was of the colour of the cap on one side and of another colour on the other. It could either be wrapped about the cap or allowed to hang free. This type of headdress was popular for mounted troops, particularly hussars in continental Europe at this period, and later in Britain. The mirleton varied somewhat in appearance from time to time, some versions having a flat top and a wide band at the bottom with a turned-up flap (peak) in front and elaborate decorations. The above specimen is black with a black and white wing. The skull-and-crossbones device and the cords, 'waffles' and tassels are white. Specimens of the mirleton are very rare. (Royal Army Museum, Stockholm.)

153: Netherlands horse artillery officer's busby, c. 1870. This is a black fur busby with a red cloth top, bag and tassel. The gilt chin chain is backed with black leather. On the front of the busby appear gilt crossed cannon and the Royal Crown. At the top front is a white plume. (Kimball P. Vickery Collection.)

154: British officer's busby, Royal Artillery, 1856–78. The silver fittings of this busby indicate that it is a volunteer officer's model. Of brown sable fur, it has a red cloth top and bag hanging over the right side. The silver plume-holder on the left side is in the form of a flaming grenade, with the Royal Artillery crest superimposed. There is a short white plume and silvered chin chain. (Wallis & Wallis.)

155: British other rank's envelope busby, Rifle Brigade, c. 1890. This headdress, adopted in 1890, is an interesting variation of the conventional busby. Sometimes called an envelope busby, it is of black fur and has black cord decorations. The front plate is the badge of the Rifle Brigade in bronze. A bronze crown appears on a black cord boss at the top front. Above the boss a bronze plume-holder in the form of a flaming grenade holds the plume. The white one shown here probably does not belong to the cap, as the Rifle Brigade had black plumes. (Norm Hobson Collection.)

156: British officer's busby, 15th Hussars, c. 1890. Yet another British busby is this black fur cap of an officer of the 18th Hussars. The blue bag has a gold trim, and there is a gold cord boss and a gilt chin chain. The tall white ostrich feather plume rises from a short red vulture feather. (Wallis & Wallis.)

157: United States busby, New York Hussars, c. 1890–1900. The busby was never adopted by the Regular United States services, except, occasionally, for bandsmen. However, it was a great favourite with some militia units, particularly those with men wealthy enough to afford costly dress uniforms. This is a black lamb's wool busby, worn by a member of Troop A, New York Hussars. The bag is yellow as is the top of the busby and the pompon at the top front. The lines and trip are in gold cord. The crossed sabres and the chin chain are of brass. (Norm Hobson Collection.)

157

158: Prussian officer's busby, 1st (Lieb) Hussars, c. 1900. This is one of the classic forms of the busby. Of brown fur, it has a silver skull-and-crossbones front plate with a silver scroll above bearing the motto 'Mit Gott Fur König und Vaterland'. The chin scales are gilt. The oval field badge at the top front of the busby is of silver metallic braid with a black velvet centre. The heron feather plume is black and white, and the top and busby bag are red cloth. An Imperial German Kokarde (black, white and red) appears under the end of the chin scales on the right side of the busby, and on the left is a black and white Kokarde (Prussia). Imperial German busbies are presently among the rarer items being sought by collectors. (Musée Royal de l'Armée, Brussels.)

159: British other rank's busby, Middlesex Yeomanry, c. 1900. The busby adopted after the Crimean War for British hussars was 7¾ inches high in front and 9 inches at the back. In 1888 this was lowered to 6¼ inches in front and 7¾ inches at the back, but the officer's plume in 1891 rose to 13 inches and by 1900 to 15 inches. The example shown here, however, is not only a trooper's but also that of a Yeomanry Hussar regiment, although it follows that of its regular counterparts in style. According to the regimental history, the Middlesex Yeomanry adopted hussar dress in 1872, but the busby bag is described as dark green and that shown here is scarlet. In other details the description follows that of the headdress illustrated – black fur, green over red brush plume and yellow lines and bosses. (Wallis & Wallis.)

160: Russian infantry officer's busby, c. 1900. The black lamb's wool body has a scarlet wool top and gilt piping. A gilt Imperial Russian double-headed eagle decorates the front. (Kimball P. Vickery Collection.)

161: United States drum major's busby, Marine Corps Band (The President's Own), c. 1912. The busby and the bearskin were never very popular in the United States except for drum majors of Army and Marine Corps bands and in a few militia and National Guard units. This tall busby is of black astrakhan, and the cloth busby top and bag are scarlet. The feather plume on the right side is coloured red, white and blue. The chin chain is gilt. (Official U.S. Marine Corps Photograph.)

159

160

161

8. The lancer cap

164

162: French Czapka of the 8th Chevau Légers Lanciers Polonais, c. 1812. The widespread employment of Lancers in European Armies was made fashionable by Napoleon. In 1807 Polish Lancers entered French service and wore the Polish uniform, including the czapka. This example lacks its plume, chin strap, and plaited line and flounders. Nonetheless it gives an idea of the prototype lancer cap, although in prints those worn by the Polish Lancers often appear taller and more waisted. The plate bearing the letter 'N' is brass but the lion's-mask bosses are plated; the fluted cloth top is green and the leather cockade is painted. The 8th Chevau-Légers-Lanciers, to whom this cap is attributed, are meant to have had a yellow top to their green upper half of the czapka. From 1808 to 1811 the regiment was the 2nd Lancer Regiment of the Vistula Legion, but in June 1811 it was incorporated, together with the 1st Vistula Lancers, into the French lancers proper. (Wallis & Wallis.)

163: British officer's lancer cap, 9th Lancers, 1832–c. 1856. The 9th Lancers, while following the rest of the Lancers in the general style of cap, had certain remarkable features of their own. The black cocktail plume shown here was first worn in 1828 but the cap itself was adopted in 1832. It incorporated the cypher of Queen Adelaide, a distinction granted in 1830. Made of black patent leather, it had gilt fittings throughout, and particular features were the rope band round the waist of the cap and the coiled rope worn as a boss for the plume. As in other regiments, the cap had a back peak permanently turned up. The trencher top was 9¾ inches square. A tailor's pattern book notes that in 1851 the sergeant major of the regiment had a private's cap plate but this and the other fittings were in gilt, not brass. (Wallis & Wallis.)

164: United States lancer cap, c. 1840. The lancer cap or czapka was never very popular in the United States. It was not worn in the Regular Army and only a very limited number of militia units ever adopted it. Shown here is a lancer cap for a now-unknown militia organisation. The skull is of deep red cloth formed over a frame. The trencher top, the band around the base of the skull and the peak or visor are of black leather, the latter being trimmed with brass. The corners of the top are decorated with small brass pieces, and gold lace runs round its four sides, as well as around the base. Gold lace also extends down the four corners. The underside of the top is covered with light tan cloth. The extra large cap plate consists of a full sunburst, upon which is superimposed an eagle, all in brass. All in all, this cap is rather flimsy. (The Smithsonian Institution.)

165: Russian lancer cap (Czapka), Imperial 14th Lancer Regiment, c. 1840–55. Examples of this extremely rare headdress are usually found only in museums or in the most advanced private collections. The cap and peak are of polished black leather. The sides of the trencher top are covered with black cloth. Silver braid extends around the top edges of the cap and down the sides. A wide silver lace band decorates the centre of the cap. The chin scales and bosses are of silvered metal. The cap plate is in the form of a semi-circular cartouche bearing the number '14'. Over the cartouche, in silvered metal, is the Imperial Russian Eagle and Crown. The shield on the eagle's breast shows St. George slaying the dragon. The plume is composed of black and white feathers. (Musée Royal de l'Armée, Brussels.)

166: Prussian officer's lancer cap (Czapka), 3rd Uhlan Regiment, Emperor Alexander of Russia's Uhlans (1st Brandenburg), c. 1844–62. The cap and peak are polished black leather. The underside of the trencher top is covered with a facing of golden yellow cloth trimmed with black cord. The gilt cap plate is in the form of a Prussian eagle with an oval cartouche on its breast bearing the initials 'FWR' (Friedrich Wilhelm Rex). The cap plate appears on the underside of the trencher top instead of on the front of the skull, as is the case with later German lancer caps. The silver cord field badge, with its black velvet centre, appears on the front left quarter of the top. The cap lines are silver cords flecked with black, ending in tassels. (Musée Royal de l'Armée, Brussels.)

165

166

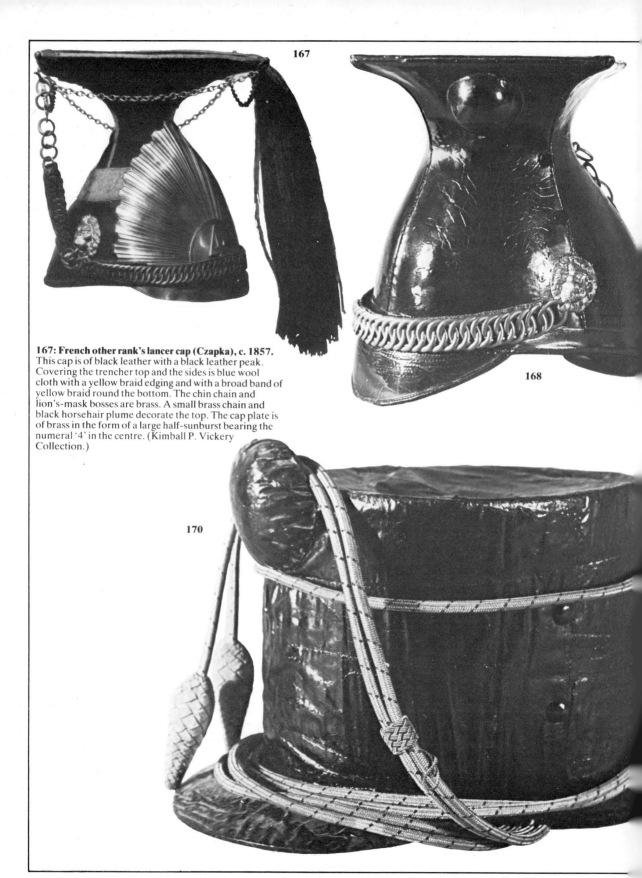

167: French other rank's lancer cap (Czapka), c. 1857.
This cap is of black leather with a black leather peak.
Covering the trencher top and the sides is blue wool
cloth with a yellow braid edging and with a broad band of
yellow braid round the bottom. The chin chain and
lion's-mask bosses are brass. A small brass chain and
black horsehair plume decorate the top. The cap plate is
of brass in the form of a large half-sunburst bearing the
numeral '4' in the centre. (Kimball P. Vickery
Collection.)

169

171: Polish lancer cap (Czapka), c. 1880. The lancer cap or czapka so popular at one time with British and European lancer units derived from the Polish konfederatka, a cloth cap with a four-sided flat top. This four-sided or trencher top gradually became characteristic of Polish military headdress. It was introduced into the French service by Polish lancer units fighting for Napoleon, and was then adopted by other armies. This later model Polish czapka is of black leather, including the peak. There is a band of red wool cloth around the base of the skull, trimmed with gold braid. The top is covered with red wool cloth trimmed about the top and bottom edges and down the corners with gold braid. A white horsehair plume adorns the left front quarter of the top. The brass cap plate is in the form of the Polish Eagle. The chin scales and bosses are brass, the latter also bearing the design of the Polish Eagle. (Norm Hobson Collection.)

171

168, 169 and 170: Officer's lightweight headdress, post-1850. At one time a removable oilcloth cover was pulled on over military headdress for use in the field and for protection from bad weather. This cover tended to make the headdress heavy and uncomfortable. Consequently, during the last half of the nineteenth century, for field use and foul weather wear, a lightweight headdress was developed which could be purchased by officers and was generally used by them. Shown here are: a British officer's lancer cap; an Austrian officer's czapka; and a British Light Dragoon officer's shako. The British officer's lancer cap has a lightweight body covered with black oilcloth. The chin chain and lion's-head bosses are gilt. The Austrian officer's czapka has a wicker body covered with green oilcloth. Its chin chain and lion's-head bosses are also gilt, while the plume is black horsehair. The British officer's shako dates from c. 1854 and also has a lightweight body covered with black oilcloth. The cap lines vary according to regiment. (Norm Hobson Collection.)

172: British other rank's lancer cap, 12th Lancer, c. 1900. This is the British Army's adaptation of the famed Polish czapka. The cap and peak are of polished black leather. The underside of the black leather top is covered with red wool cloth, with a stripe of blue between two stripes of yellow round the bottom. A brass ornament appears at all four corners of the top, with a yellow stripe running down from each of them. On the left front quarter of the top appears a blue and yellow wool rosette bearing a regimental button, and above it is a brass plume-holder with a red plume. The chin chain and bosses are of brass. The large, elaborate triangular front plate bears the Royal Arms, the plume, coronet and motto of the Prince of Wales, as well as the battle honours of the 12th Lancers. (Wallis & Wallis.)

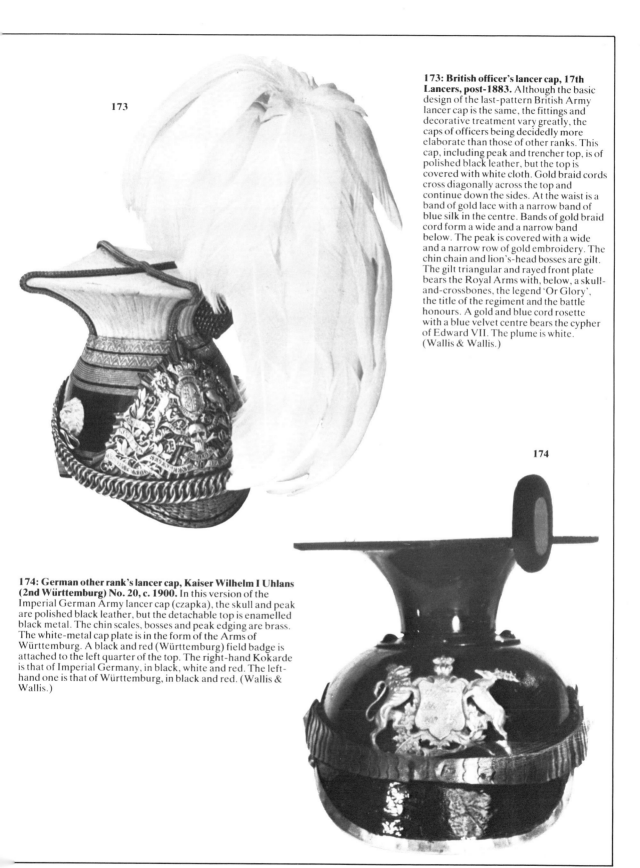

173

173: British officer's lancer cap, 17th Lancers, post-1883. Although the basic design of the last-pattern British Army lancer cap is the same, the fittings and decorative treatment vary greatly, the caps of officers being decidedly more elaborate than those of other ranks. This cap, including peak and trencher top, is of polished black leather, but the top is covered with white cloth. Gold braid cords cross diagonally across the top and continue down the sides. At the waist is a band of gold lace with a narrow band of blue silk in the centre. Bands of gold braid cord form a wide and a narrow band below. The peak is covered with a wide and a narrow row of gold embroidery. The chin chain and lion's-head bosses are gilt. The gilt triangular and rayed front plate bears the Royal Arms with, below, a skull-and-crossbones, the legend 'Or Glory', the title of the regiment and the battle honours. A gold and blue cord rosette with a blue velvet centre bears the cypher of Edward VII. The plume is white. (Wallis & Wallis.)

174

174: German other rank's lancer cap, Kaiser Wilhelm I Uhlans (2nd Württemburg) No. 20, c. 1900. In this version of the Imperial German Army lancer cap (czapka), the skull and peak are polished black leather, but the detachable top is enamelled black metal. The chin scales, bosses and peak edging are brass. The white-metal cap plate is in the form of the Arms of Württemburg. A black and red (Württemburg) field badge is attached to the left quarter of the top. The right-hand Kokarde is that of Imperial Germany, in black, white and red. The left-hand one is that of Württemburg, in black and red. (Wallis & Wallis.)

175: British officer's lancer cap, 9th Lancers, post-1901. The regimental peculiarities noted for the 9th Lancers cap of 1832–56 (Plate 163) were continued in the last-pattern full dress headdress worn by the regiment. Still of black patent leather and with gilt fittings, this style of cap, with its smaller waist and lower crown, was sealed in 1856 and although it changed slightly in shape during the remainder of the century (the profile of the front plate, in particular, becoming less sloping), its basic specifications of $6\frac{1}{2}$ inches high in front rising to $8\frac{1}{2}$ inches at the back were constant. The best dating guides are the battle honours, which accumulated on the rayed plate, and the adoption of the low-arched crown, the so-called King's Crown, in 1901 (as shown here). In 1875 black and white cocktail plumes were ordered for the 9th in Review Order and at Levées, or black horsehair in other orders of dress. Other ranks, whose cap embodied similar regimental features, also had a black horsehair plume. The 1900 Dress Regulations gave the plumes of the other Lancer regiments as green for the 5th, scarlet for the 12th, black for the 16th, and white for the 17th and 21st. (Wallis & Wallis.)

176: Prussian Uhlan officer's lancer cap (Czapka), c. 1910. The skull, top and peak are all black leather. The chin scales, peak edging and cap plate are gilt. The plate is the Prussian heraldic line eagle with a ribbon across the wings bearing the motto 'Mit Gott Fur König und Vaterland'. The initials 'FR' (Friedrich Rex) appear on the eagle's breast. On the left front quarter of the trencher top is a field badge of silver cord with a black velvet centre. The cap lines, which are of silver flecked with black, hang with silver tassels from the right front quarter of the top. The right Kokarde is that of Imperial Germany, the left one is that of Prussia. (Walter Hartman Collection.)

177: Austrian officer's lancer cap (Czapka), 3rd Uhlan Regiment, c. 1910. The cap is lower and the top is much smaller than was the case with the lancer caps of other armies. The polished black leather skull has a black leather top and peak. The latter is decorated with a wide band of gold embroidery. The chin scales are gilt, as are the bosses. The top, both above and underneath, is covered with maroon

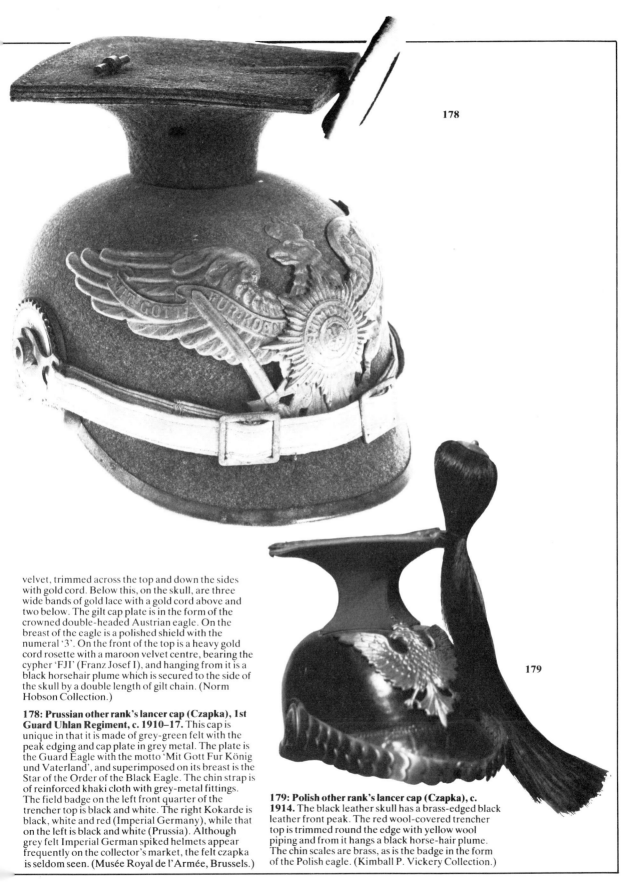

178

179

velvet, trimmed across the top and down the sides with gold cord. Below this, on the skull, are three wide bands of gold lace with a gold cord above and two below. The gilt cap plate is in the form of the crowned double-headed Austrian eagle. On the breast of the eagle is a polished shield with the numeral '3'. On the front of the top is a heavy gold cord rosette with a maroon velvet centre, bearing the cypher 'FJI' (Franz Josef I), and hanging from it is a black horsehair plume which is secured to the side of the skull by a double length of gilt chain. (Norm Hobson Collection.)

178: Prussian other rank's lancer cap (Czapka), 1st Guard Uhlan Regiment, c. 1910–17. This cap is unique in that it is made of grey-green felt with the peak edging and cap plate in grey metal. The plate is the Guard Eagle with the motto 'Mit Gott Fur König und Vaterland', and superimposed on its breast is the Star of the Order of the Black Eagle. The chin strap is of reinforced khaki cloth with grey-metal fittings. The field badge on the left front quarter of the trencher top is black and white. The right Kokarde is black, white and red (Imperial Germany), while that on the left is black and white (Prussia). Although grey felt Imperial German spiked helmets appear frequently on the collector's market, the felt czapka is seldom seen. (Musée Royal de l'Armée, Brussels.)

179: Polish other rank's lancer cap (Czapka), c. 1914. The black leather skull has a brass-edged black leather front peak. The red wool-covered trencher top is trimmed round the edge with yellow wool piping and from it hangs a black horse-hair plume. The chin scales are brass, as is the badge in the form of the Polish eagle. (Kimball P. Vickery Collection.)

9. Tropical helmets

180

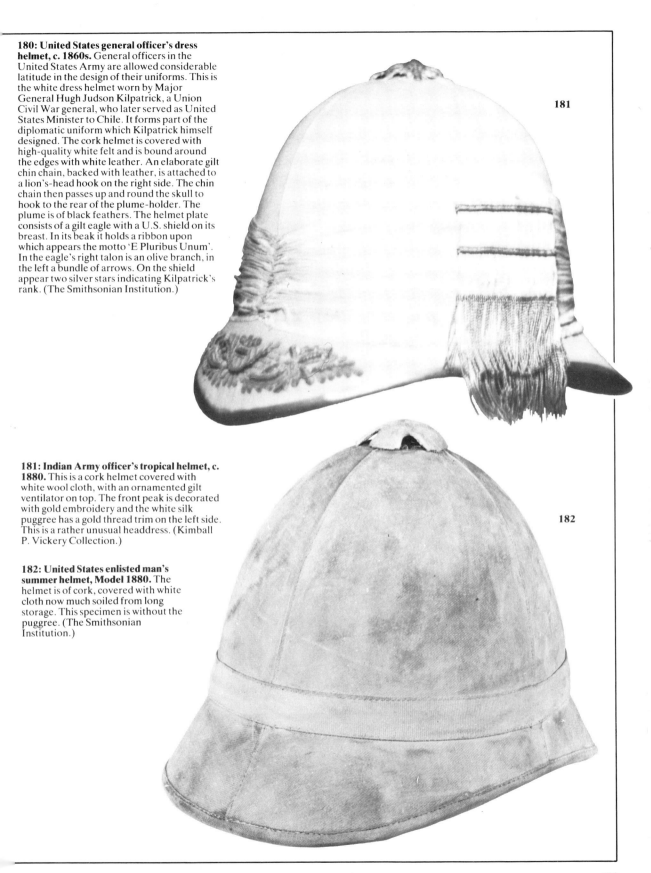

180: United States general officer's dress helmet, c. 1860s. General officers in the United States Army are allowed considerable latitude in the design of their uniforms. This is the white dress helmet worn by Major General Hugh Judson Kilpatrick, a Union Civil War general, who later served as United States Minister to Chile. It forms part of the diplomatic uniform which Kilpatrick himself designed. The cork helmet is covered with high-quality white felt and is bound around the edges with white leather. An elaborate gilt chin chain, backed with leather, is attached to a lion's-head hook on the right side. The chin chain then passes up and round the skull to hook to the rear of the plume-holder. The plume is of black feathers. The helmet plate consists of a gilt eagle with a U.S. shield on its breast. In its beak it holds a ribbon upon which appears the motto 'E Pluribus Unum'. In the eagle's right talon is an olive branch, in the left a bundle of arrows. On the shield appear two silver stars indicating Kilpatrick's rank. (The Smithsonian Institution.)

181

181: Indian Army officer's tropical helmet, c. 1880. This is a cork helmet covered with white wool cloth, with an ornamented gilt ventilator on top. The front peak is decorated with gold embroidery and the white silk puggree has a gold thread trim on the left side. This is a rather unusual headdress. (Kimball P. Vickery Collection.)

182: United States enlisted man's summer helmet, Model 1880. The helmet is of cork, covered with white cloth now much soiled from long storage. This specimen is without the puggree. (The Smithsonian Institution.)

182

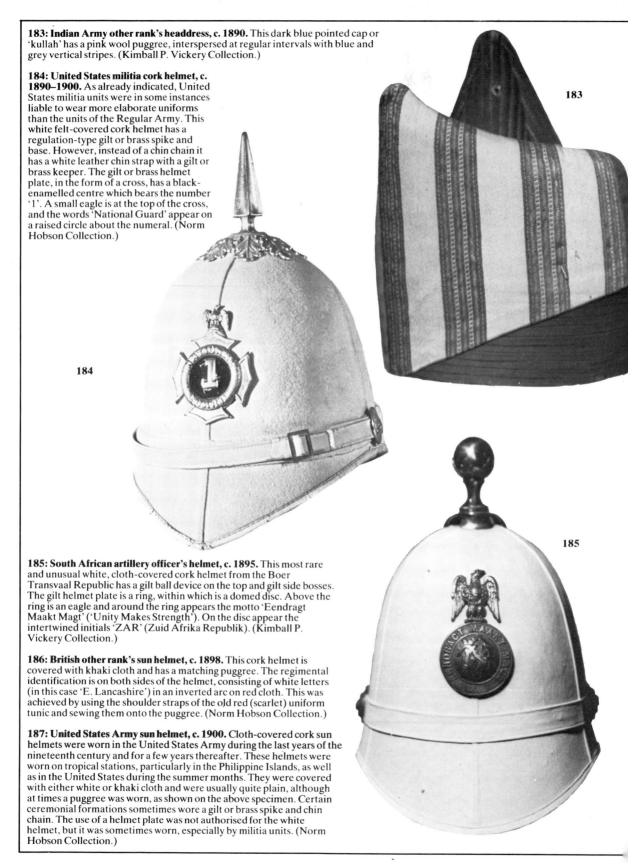

183: Indian Army other rank's headdress, c. 1890. This dark blue pointed cap or 'kullah' has a pink wool puggree, interspersed at regular intervals with blue and grey vertical stripes. (Kimball P. Vickery Collection.)

183

184: United States militia cork helmet, c. 1890–1900. As already indicated, United States militia units were in some instances liable to wear more elaborate uniforms than the units of the Regular Army. This white felt-covered cork helmet has a regulation-type gilt or brass spike and base. However, instead of a chin chain it has a white leather chin strap with a gilt or brass keeper. The gilt or brass helmet plate, in the form of a cross, has a black-enamelled centre which bears the number '1'. A small eagle is at the top of the cross, and the words 'National Guard' appear on a raised circle about the numeral. (Norm Hobson Collection.)

184

185

185: South African artillery officer's helmet, c. 1895. This most rare and unusual white, cloth-covered cork helmet from the Boer Transvaal Republic has a gilt ball device on the top and gilt side bosses. The gilt helmet plate is a ring, within which is a domed disc. Above the ring is an eagle and around the ring appears the motto 'Eendragt Maakt Magt' ('Unity Makes Strength'). On the disc appear the intertwined initials 'ZAR' (Zuid Afrika Republik). (Kimball P. Vickery Collection.)

186: British other rank's sun helmet, c. 1898. This cork helmet is covered with khaki cloth and has a matching puggree. The regimental identification is on both sides of the helmet, consisting of white letters (in this case 'E. Lancashire') in an inverted arc on red cloth. This was achieved by using the shoulder straps of the old red (scarlet) uniform tunic and sewing them onto the puggree. (Norm Hobson Collection.)

187: United States Army sun helmet, c. 1900. Cloth-covered cork sun helmets were worn in the United States Army during the last years of the nineteenth century and for a few years thereafter. These helmets were worn on tropical stations, particularly in the Philippine Islands, as well as in the United States during the summer months. They were covered with either white or khaki cloth and were usually quite plain, although at times a puggree was worn, as shown on the above specimen. Certain ceremonial formations sometimes wore a gilt or brass spike and chin chain. The use of a helmet plate was not authorised for the white helmet, but it was sometimes worn, especially by militia units. (Norm Hobson Collection.)

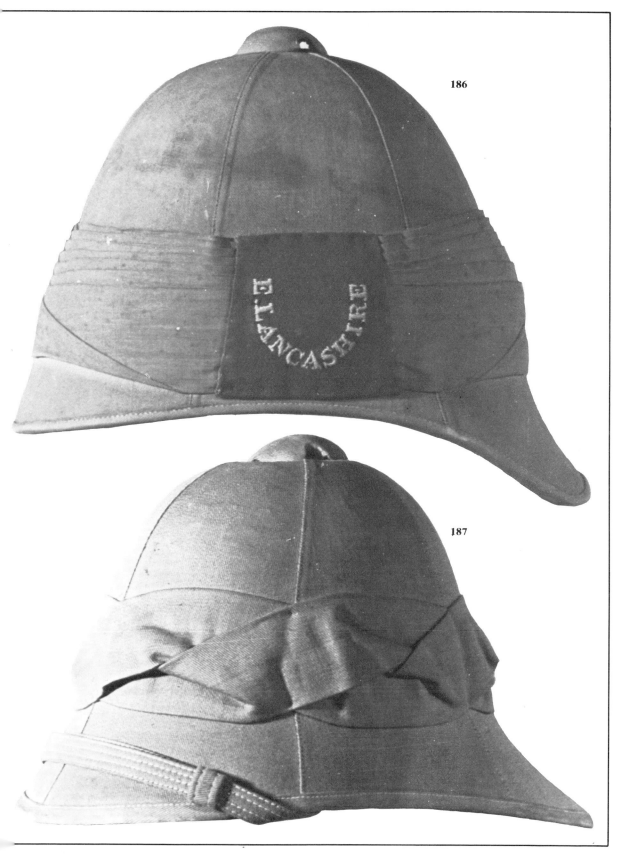

186

187

188: British other rank's tropical helmet, Civil Service Volunteer Rifle Corps, c. 1901–08. The cork helmet is covered with grey cloth, bound round the edges with black leather. The white-metal badge is a Maltese Cross surmounted by a crown. A ring in the centre of the cross bears the name of the unit in raised letters. The Prince of Wales's plume and coronet appear in the centre of the badge. (Norm Hobson Collection.)

188

189: German other rank's tropical helmet, c. 1914. Tropical headdress is extremely rare and marks a field only recently being developed by collectors. This Imperial German cork helmet was worn in Asia and East Africa. The grey-metal helmet plate is the Imperial German eagle, not the Prussian eagle. (The Smithsonian Institution.)

189

190: German infantry tropical helmet, c. 1914. This rare cork helmet is covered with tan cloth and has a grey-metal spike and base. It is lined with green felt. There is no provision for a chin strap or Kokarden. The regimental number '7' on the front of the helmet is of red wool cloth. (Norm Hobson Collection.)

191: German officer's tropical helmet, c. 1914. The helmet is of cork, covered with khaki cloth. The helmet plate, trim and spike base are of gilt-metal. The Imperial Kokarde on the right side is in black, white and red. There is no State (Land) Kokarde for the reason already mentioned in comments on Plate 241. The spike base will accommodate either a spike or a plume. This type of helmet is extremely rare. (The Smithsonian Institution.)

190

191

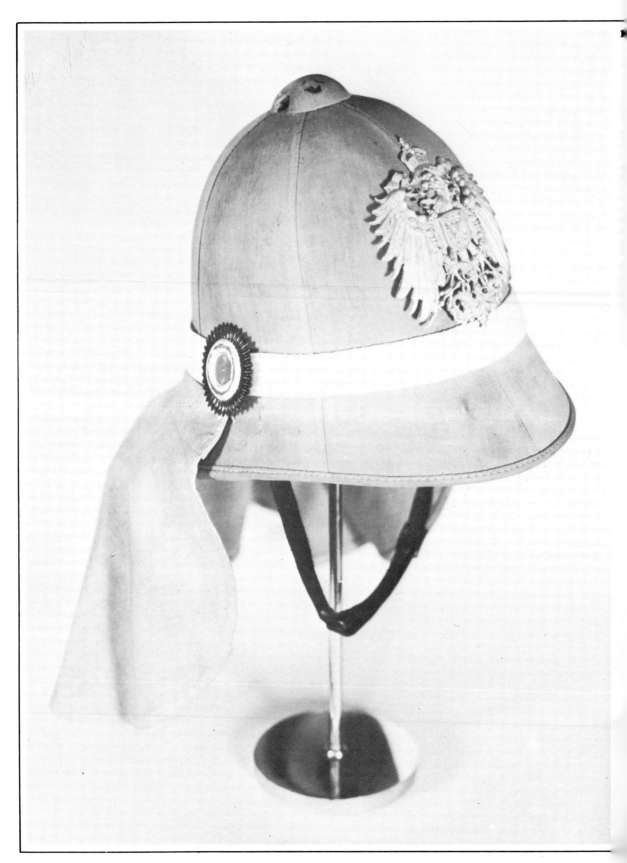

2: German infantry other rank's tropical
...met, c. 1914. This cork helmet is covered with
... cloth and there is a white band (indicating
...antry) around the base of the skull. A tan spine
...th is attached to the helmet under the white
...d. The chin strap is of brown leather. The
...gle Kokarde, on the right side, is of stamped
...tal and is in the Imperial colours of black,
...ite and red. (Norm Hobson Collection.)

3: German tropical helmet, c. 1914. Still
...other Imperial German tropical helmet. This
...k helmet is covered with white cloth, but
...mples are known with a tan cloth cover. The
...all grey-metal helmet plate bears the
...imental number. There is a grey-metal spike
...e but no spike as such was worn. The white
...ne cloth is attached to the helmet by a brown
...ther strap. There is no provision for a chin
...ap or for Kokarden. This helmet was worn in
...rld War One in Mesopotamia. (Norm Hobson
...lection.)

4: Belgian non-commissioned officer's
...pical helmet, c. 1914. This helmet, worn by the
...lic Force of the Belgian Congo, is of cork,
...ered with khaki cloth and with a khaki pugree.
...e bronze-metal badge shows the Belgium lion
...rounded by two laurel branches and
...mounted by the Royal Crown. The officers
...l gold helmet plates. The Public Force was
...ninistered by the Belgian Ministry of Colonies
... the officers and some non-commissioned
...cers were seconded from the Belgian Army to
... Force. Other non-commissioned officers and
...other ranks were Congolese. (The
...ithsonian Institution.)

193

194

10. Caps

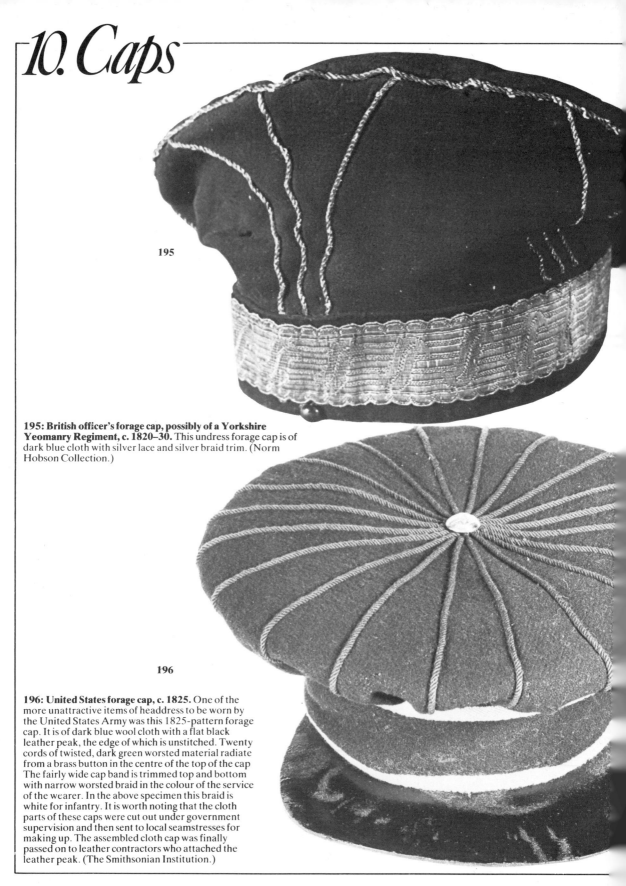

195: British officer's forage cap, possibly of a Yorkshire Yeomanry Regiment, c. 1820–30. This undress forage cap is of dark blue cloth with silver lace and silver braid trim. (Norm Hobson Collection.)

196: United States forage cap, c. 1825. One of the more unattractive items of headdress to be worn by the United States Army was this 1825-pattern forage cap. It is of dark blue wool cloth with a flat black leather peak, the edge of which is unstitched. Twenty cords of twisted, dark green worsted material radiate from a brass button in the centre of the top of the cap The fairly wide cap band is trimmed top and bottom with narrow worsted braid in the colour of the service of the wearer. In the above specimen this braid is white for infantry. It is worth noting that the cloth parts of these caps were cut out under government supervision and then sent to local seamstresses for making up. The assembled cloth cap was finally passed on to leather contractors who attached the leather peak. (The Smithsonian Institution.)

197

197: United States forage cap, 1833–39.
This black all-leather forage cap certainly
lacks 'style'. In addition to being worn by
the United States Army, this cap was worn
by cadets at the United States Military
Academy, and specimens in the latter's
museum indicate that a modified version
of it was worn by some militia units. The
cap is designed to fold nearly flat. The
above example is devoid of all decoration
although there is some evidence that a
yellow-metal ornament in the form of a
Company initial may have been worn.
(The Smithsonian Institution.)

198

**198: United States militia version forage
cap, 1833–39.** The above headdress is
another militia version of the United
States Army forage cap shown in Plate 46.
Instead of being made of leather,
however, the body of the cap is made of
cardboard, covered with grey wool cloth.
Except for a few fragments, most of this
cloth covering is missing from the front of
the cap. The peak or visor and the trim are
of black leather. At the top front of the cap
is a brass cap plate in the form of a light
infantry bugle suspended from three cords
tied in three bows. This plate is enclosed
by a design in black braid. A brass star
decorates the bottom front of the cap.
(West Point Museum Collections.)

199

200

199: United States enlisted man's fatigue cap, 1839. Of dark blue cloth, this cap has a black leather peak or visor. A 'cape' is stitched to the rear half of the cap. When not in use, in bad weather, this cape was folded up, as shown here, and was held in place by the chin strap buttons and by cloth tape passing across the front of the cap. In some instances a coloured and detachable band was worn around the cap. The colour varied according to the arm of the wearer, i.e., red for artillery, white for infantry, yellow for dragoons and sky blue for ordnance. Cadets at the United States Military Academy wore this cap with a detachable black velvet band with the letter's 'USMA' in modified Old English script within a wreath of olive and laurel, all in gold embroidery. The convex black leather peak is not stitched. The black leather chin strap is attached to each side of the cap with brass buttons bearing the U.S. eagle and shield. (The Smithsonian Institution.)

200: United States officer's fatigue cap, 1839. The officer's model of the 1839 fatigue cap is of much better quality and the peak or visor is more horizontal. (West Point Museum Collections.)

201: United States forage cap, New Hampshire Militia, c. 1840. This cap is very similar to the United States Army leather forage cap of 1833–39 (Plate 46), but has been dressed up by the addition of a brass cap plate, a brass strap across the lower front of the cap, and by brass buttons. The cap plate is rectangular, with four scallops top and bottom. There is a floral border about the plate. Within the border, in the centre of the plate, is an eagle with outspread wings and a U.S. shield on its breast. Above the eagle, on a ribbon, is the motto 'E Pluribus Unum' and thirteen five-pointed stars. The eagle is superimposed on a trophy of arms and flags. (West Point Museum Collections.)

201

202

202: Canadian militia officer's undress cap, c. 1845–50. The dark blue cloth cap, with its soft padded crown, has a black leather chin strap and black leather peak. Around the cap is an embroidered black band with an oak-leaf and acorn design. At the front appears a silver-embroidered crowned 'VR' (Victoria Regina cypher. A similar cap was worn in the British Army during this period. (Manitoba Museum of Man & Nature.)

203

204

203: Canadian officer's pillbox cap, North West Mounted Police, post-1875. This pillbox cap for officer's undress wear is similar to that worn by British Army officers and by United States Marine officers of the period. The blue peakless cap has a gold braid trim with a gold net button on top, gold braid decorative design, and a black leather chin strap. Apparently it was not a very popular item in any of the services. (Glenbow-Alberta Institute.)

204: Canadian officer's undress forage cap, 13th Royal Canadian Militia, c. 1867. The cap is of dark blue cloth with a scarlet band and has a black leather peak. On the top are a black net button and decorative loops. The cap device, in gold embroidery, consists of the number '13' within an oval bearing the legend 'Royal Canadian Militia', around which is a wreath and a crown on top. This cap is similar to the undress forage cap worn by officers of the British Army of that period. (Manitoba Museum of Man & Nature.)

205: Indian Army other rank's pillbox cap, c. 1870. This red wool cap is decorated with a blue band round the bottom and with narrow blue braid dividing the cap into quarters. On the front appears the brass numeral '2'. (Kimball P. Vickery Collection.)

205

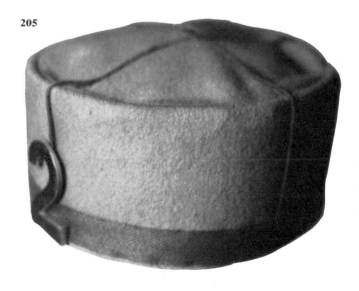

206: Canadian militia officer's undress forage cap, late nineteenth century. The dark blue body has a wide, silver-embroidered band bearing a motif of oak-leaves and acorns. The top has a silver net button and eight small silver braid decorative loops. The black leather peak is decorated with a wide band of silver embroidery. (Manitoba Museum of Man & Nature.)

207: British officer's peaked forage cap, c. 1890. This cap is of black wool with a black leather peak, trimmed with a wide band of silver embroidery. A wide band of figured silver lace surrounds the base of the cap and the top is decorated with a knot of silver braid. Silver lace is normally associated with Volunteers, whereas, broadly speaking, gold lace was reserved for Regulars. (Kimball P. Vickery Collection.)

208: British officer's pillbox cap, probably Royal Artillery, c. 1890. This cap, of black wool, has a wide band of figured gold lace round the bottom. The top is decorated with a gold braid knot. (Kimball P. Vickery Collection.)

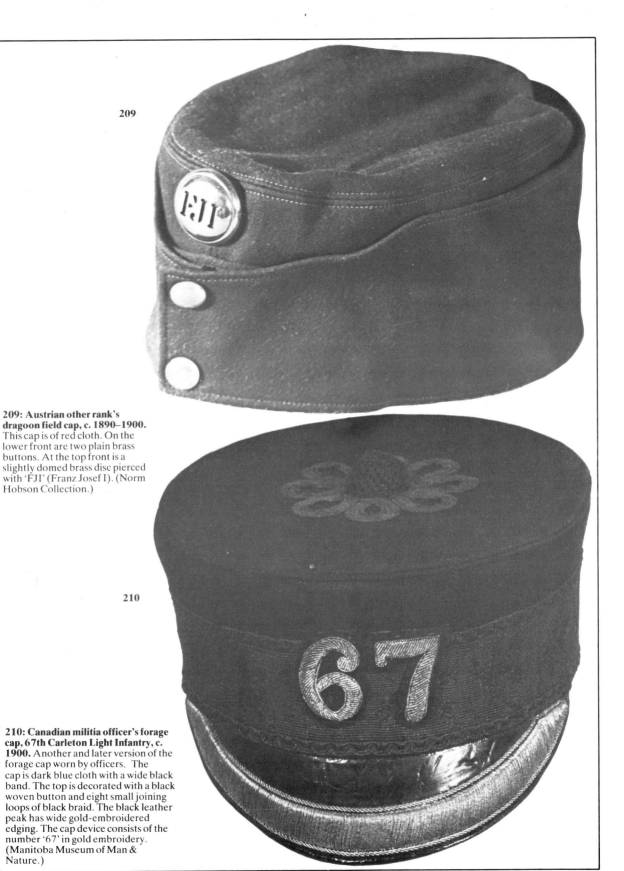

209

209: Austrian other rank's dragoon field cap, c. 1890–1900. This cap is of red cloth. On the lower front are two plain brass buttons. At the top front is a slightly domed brass disc pierced with 'FJI' (Franz Josef I). (Norm Hobson Collection.)

210

210: Canadian militia officer's forage cap, 67th Carleton Light Infantry, c. 1900. Another and later version of the forage cap worn by officers. The cap is dark blue cloth with a wide black band. The top is decorated with a black woven button and eight small joining loops of black braid. The black leather peak has wide gold-embroidered edging. The cap device consists of the number '67' in gold embroidery. (Manitoba Museum of Man & Nature.)

211: United States enlisted man's bell-crown cap, c. 1907. This is the Model 1902 cap with the Field Artillery cap device authorised in 1907. The cap is of dark blue cloth with a black leather chin strap and a black leather peak or visor. There is a brass buckle on the chin strap and it is secured to each side of the cap by a small brass button bearing the Arms of the U.S. Around the top and bottom of the cap band is a narrow red felt band. Red is the artillery 'colour'. (The colour of the narrow bands and the cap device varied according to arm or service.) The crossed cannons denoting Field Artillery have a figure '1' above and the letter 'A' below, indicating that the wearer was a member of Battery A of the 1st U.S. Field Artillery. A similar cap was also worn by National Guard troops. (The Smithsonian Institution.)

211

212

213

212: British officer's forage cap, Royal Welsh Fusiliers, c. 1900. This dark blue wool cap has a gold embroidered flaming grenade on the left front. At the front, in a vertical line on the flaps, which are turned back against the cap, are two gilt regimental buttons bearing the Prince of Wales's coronet and plume. (Kimball P. Vickery Collection.)

213: Austrian artillery officer's field cap, c. 1910. This cap is made of soft field grey cloth. At the top front is a gold cord cockade with maroon centre, bearing the cypher of Franz Josef. The two gilt buttons at the front bear crossed cannons. (Kimball P. Vickery Collection.)

214: United States Marine Corps officer's full dress caps, c. 1912. The upper cap is that of the Major General Commandant. It is dark blue, and the peak or visor is decorated with a gold-embroidered oak-leaf wreath. A gold-embroidered oak-leaf and acorn band encircles the back and sides of the cap. On the top of the cap is a gold-embroidered quatrefoil, and on the front is a silver and gold Marine Corps emblem within a gold-embroidered wreath. On the emblem the silver globe shows the North and South American continents in gold. Behind the globe is a gold fouled anchor and on top of it is a silver eagle. The chin strap is of gold lace with a red stripe in the centre. The gold buttons on the side of the cap bear the Marine Corps emblem and thirteen stars, one for each of the thirteen original colonies. The lower cap, also elaborately decorated, is that of a field grade officer. Basically similar to that of the Commandant, it has a simpler motif of oak-leaves and acorns on the visor. The chin strap and the quatrefoil on top of the cap are the same, as are the side buttons. The Marine Corps emblem at the front of the cap is without the embroidered wreath and instead of the gold-embroidered oak-leaves and acorns about the cap band, there is a wide band of gold lace. (Official Marine Corps Photograph.)

214

215

216

215: German other rank's field cap, c. 1910. This cloth field cap (Feldmutze), was worn by German other ranks when the helmet or other headdress was not prescribed. The colour of the cap and piping varied according to the regiment and service, as did the cap band. The above specimen is a blue cap with red (infantry) piping and band. The upper Kokarde is in the Imperial colours of black, white and red. The lower Kokarde is in the colour of the wearer's State (Land). In this instance the Kokarde is yellow and red (Baden). (Norm Hobson Collection.)

216: Prussian other rank's oilcloth field cap, c. 1914. Among the rarer Imperial German other ranks headdress is the oilcloth field cap (Feldmutze). Most often seen are those of Prussia, Bavaria and Saxony. These were worn by Landwehr units early in World War One, and the one shown above is from a Prussian unit. The black oil-cloth cap generally resembles the German field cap of the period. The large brass Landwehr cross is held to the cap by black thread, as is the Prussian Kokarde in black and white. (Norm Hobson Collection.)

217

217: Serbian infantry officer's peak cap, c. 1912. The field grey wool body, with its thin black leather peak, has red piping round the top. On the front is a badge composed of the Serbian double-headed eagle and crown, within a wreath. This badge is of gilt, with a red velvet background. (Kimball P. Vickery Collection.)

218: German oilcloth field cap, c. 1914. This is another example of the oilcloth field cap worn early in World War One by Imperial German troops. This specimen is of black oilcloth with a polished black leather peak. The cap plate is in the form of a large Landwehr cross with the motto 'Mit Gott Fur Koenig und Vaterland and the date '1913'. Under the cross is a small metal Kokarde in the Imperial German colours of black, white and red. Examples of the peaked oilcloth cap also appear in grey oilcloth, and are known to have been worn by Prussian, Saxon and Bavarian Landwehr units. (Norm Hobson Collection.)

219: British officer's forage cap, Corps of Royal Engineers, c. 1914. This cap is of khaki cotton cloth and the peak is covered with the same material. The chin strap is of tan leather. An unusual feature is the cape at the rear, which fastens across the front by a tan cloth strap with metal eyelets and a buckle. This cape may be turned down to protect the back of the neck. On the front of the cap are the badge of the Royal Engineers and the Royal Cypher within the Garter, all enclosed within a laurel wreath. On top of the Garter is a crown. Across the lower portion of the wreath is a scroll bearing the words 'Royal Engineers'. (Kimball P. Vickery Collection.)

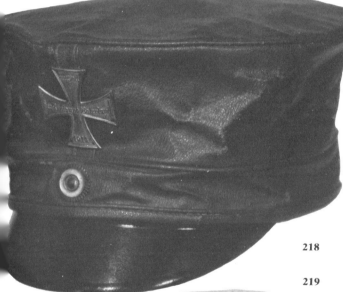

218

219

11. Storage cases and cap covers

220

220: British officer's Home Service helmet, 1878 pattern, and storage box. The officer's name and the name of his regiment, in this case the post-1881 title of the East Surrey Regiment, are engraved on a brass plate on the top front of the japanned tin case. There is an increasing interest among collectors in these storage or shipping cases and it is most desirable to find them together with the proper helmet. (Norm Hobson Collection.)

221: German (Württemburg) officer's helmet and case, early 1900s.
The conical fibreboard case is fitted with a leather carrying strap. The black leather helmet has a gilt spike, helmet plate, chin scales and peak edging. The helmet plate shows the Arms of Wurttemburg. The right Kokarde (Imperial) is black, white and red, and that on the left (Württemburg) is black and red. This is a set much sought after by collectors. (Norm Hobson Collection.)

221

222, 223 and 224: United States 9th Infantry officer's helmet, with storage case, 1881. The United States services used a tole storage or shipping case similar to the British type. These three illustrations show: an officer's helmet of the 9th United States Infantry; the helmet with spike removed (and placed under the helmet) resting in the case; and the case closed. All fittings are of excellent-quality gilt, with the exception of the regimental number which is of silver. Crossed rifles behind the shield on the helmet plate and on the side buttons identify it as an infantry helmet. The covering of this cork helmet is of extremely good-quality black cloth. (The Smithsonian Institution.)

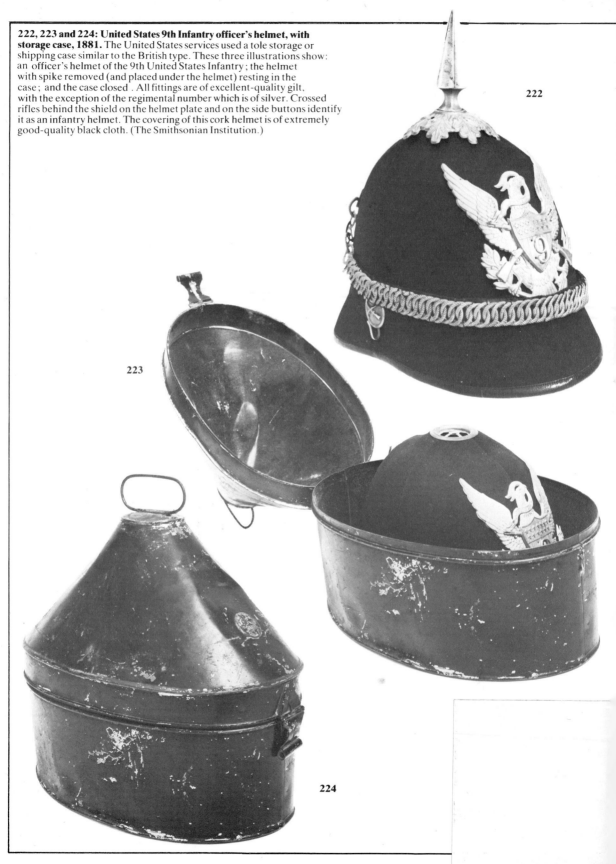

222

223

224

225: Austrian artillery officer's shako, with case, pre-1914. Another interesting combination is this pre-World War One shako with its heavy black leather shipping or carrying case. The black felt shako is decorated with gold lace and gold braid. The chin chain is also of gilt, as are the bosses. The gilt shako plate is in the form of the crowned Austrian double-headed eagle with the Austrian Arms on its breast. The black horsehair plume hangs from a gold cord button bearing the cypher 'FJI' (Franz Josef I). (Norm Hobson Collection.)

226: German other rank's Pickelhaube and cover, c. 1914. Cloth Picklehaube covers were introduced into the Imperial German service as early as 1892. Some of these were plain, as in the example shown here for an other rank's helmet. Others bore a distinguishing device, including some who had the regimental number in red on the front, and the Landsturm Infantry Regiments who had the Landwehr cross in red. These are but two of several examples. At the end of 1914 all distinguishing devices were removed since such an arrangement made the identification of units too easy for enemy intelligence experts. (Norm Flayderman Collection.)

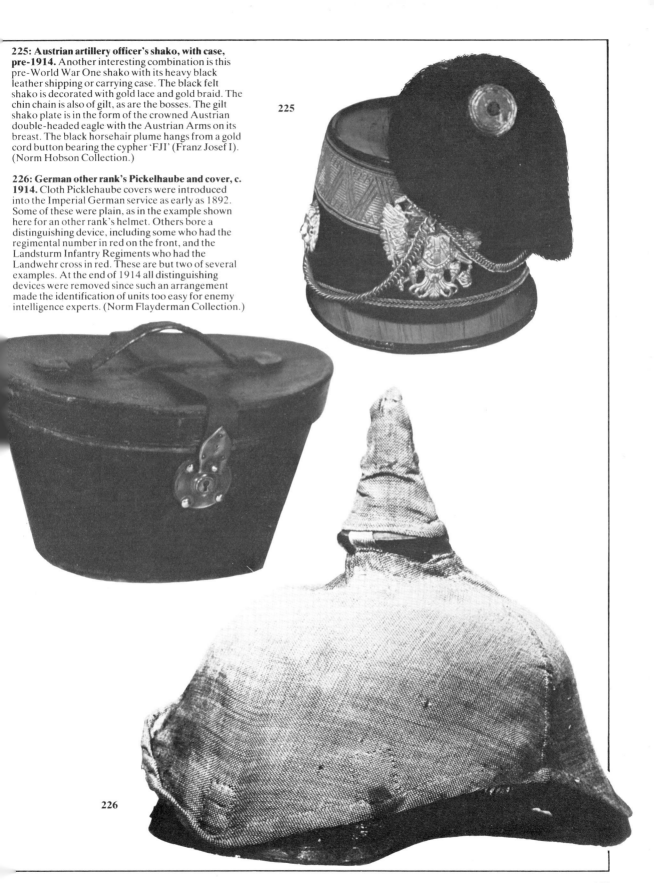

225

226

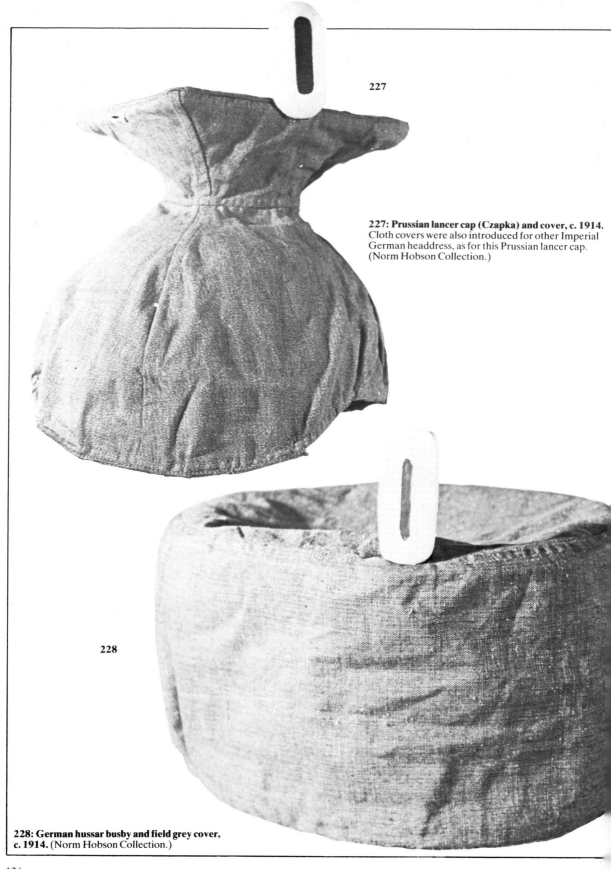

227

227: Prussian lancer cap (Czapka) and cover, c. 1914.
Cloth covers were also introduced for other Imperial
German headdress, as for this Prussian lancer cap.
(Norm Hobson Collection.)

228

**228: German hussar busby and field grey cover,
c. 1914.** (Norm Hobson Collection.)

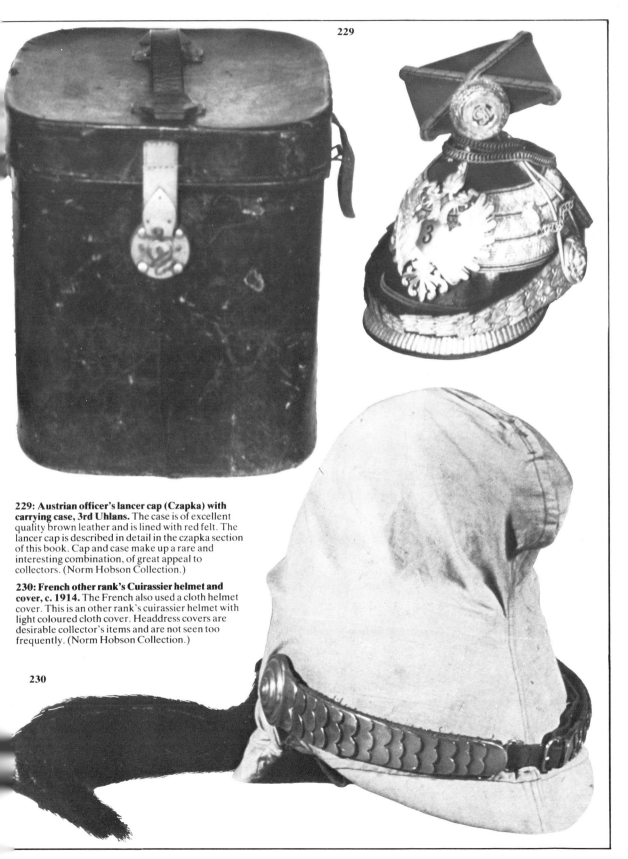

229

229: Austrian officer's lancer cap (Czapka) with carrying case, 3rd Uhlans. The case is of excellent quality brown leather and is lined with red felt. The lancer cap is described in detail in the czapka section of this book. Cap and case make up a rare and interesting combination, of great appeal to collectors. (Norm Hobson Collection.)

230: French other rank's Cuirassier helmet and cover, c. 1914. The French also used a cloth helmet cover. This is an other rank's cuirassier helmet with light coloured cloth cover. Headdress covers are desirable collector's items and are not seen too frequently. (Norm Hobson Collection.)

230

Bibliography

Books

BARNES, Major R. Money, *A History of the Regiments and Uniforms of the British Army*. London: Seeley Service & Co., Ltd. 1951.

BARNES, Major R. Money, *Military Uniforms of Britain and the Empire*. London: Seeley Service & Co., Ltd. 1960.

CAMPBELL, J. Duncan and HOWELL, Edgar M., *American Military Insignia 1800–1851*. Washington: Smithsonian Institution. 1963.

CARMAN, William Y., *Head Dresses of the British Army – Cavalry*. Sutton, Surrey: W. Y. Carman. 1968.

CARMAN, William Y., *Headdresses of the British Army – Yeomanry*. Sutton, Surrey: W. Y. Carman. 1970.

CHAPPELL, Gordon, *Brass Spikes & Horsehair Plumes*. Tucson: Arizona Pioneers' Historical Society. 1966.

CHAPPELL, Gordon, *Summer Helmets of the U.S. Army 1875–1910*. Cheyenne: The Wyoming State Archives and Historical Department. 1967.

CHAPPELL, Gordon, *The Search for the Well-Dressed Soldier*. Tucson: Arizona Historical Society. 1972.

CURTIS, John Obed and Guthman, William H., *New England Militia Uniforms and Accoutrements*. Sturbridge: Old Sturbridge Village. 1971.

EDWARDS, Major T. J., *Regimental Badges*. Aldershot: Gale & Polden Limited. 1951.

GROSVENOR, Gilbert, and others, *Insignia and Decorations of the U.S. Armed Forces*. Washington: National Geographic Society. 1944.

Home Service Helmets 1878–1914, with Regimental Plates. London: Star Products. No date.

HOWELL, Edgar M. and KLOSTER, Donald E., *United States Army Headgear to 1854*. Washington: Smithsonian Institution Press. 1969.

KANNIK, Preben, edited by Carman, William Y. *Military Uniforms in Colour*. London: Blandford Press. 1968.

KILMA, Herbert, (English translation by Richard K. Riehn) *Helmets of Military Formations and Civil Guard Units in Austria-Hungary, c. 1900*. Munich: Graf Klenan. 1971.

LORD, Francis A. and WISE, Arthur, *Uniforms of the Civil War*. South Brunswick: Thomas Yoseloff. 1970.

MELEGARI, Vezio, *The World's Great Regiments*. New York: G. P. Putnam's Sons. 1969.

MOLLO, John, *Military Fashion*. New York: G. P. Putnam's Sons. 1972.

MULLER, Henrich and KUNTER, Fritz, *Europaische Helme*. Berlin: Militarverlag der Deutschen Demokratischen Republik. No date.

PIETSCH, Paul, *Die Formations und Uniformierungs–Geschichte des preubischen Heeres 1080 bis 1914*. Hamburg: Verlag Helmut Gerhard Schulz. (Two volumes, 1963 and 1966.)

RANKIN, Colonel Robert H., *Uniforms of the Sea Services*. Annapolis: U.S. Naval Institute. 1962.

RANKIN, Colonel Robert H., *Helmets and Headdress of the Imperial German Army 1870–1918*. New Milford: N. Flayderman & Co. 1965.

RANKIN, Colonel Robert H., *Uniforms of the Army*. New York: G. P. Putnam's Sons. 1967.

RANKIN, Colonel Robert H., *Uniforms of the Marines*. New York: G. P. Putnam's Sons. 1970

WERLICH, Robert, *Orders and Decorations of All Nations*. Washington: Quaker Press. 1965.

WILKINSON, Frederick, *Battle Dress*. Garden City: Doubleday & Company. 1970.

WILKINSON-LATHAM, Robert and Christopher, *Cavalry Uniforms of Britain and the Commonwealth*. New York: The Macmillan Company. 1970.

Articles

GIBELLINI, Lt. Col. V., 'The Grenadiers of the Guard of the Duchy of Parma, 1851'. *Tradition*, No. 48, pp 2–3.

HEFTER, Joseph, 'Chronicle of Military Dress in Mexico, XVI to XX Century'. *Artes de Mexico*, No. 102. 1968.

HUNT, Donald, 'The Bavarian Hartschieres'. *Tradition*, No. 47, pp 14–16.

HUNT, Donald, 'Sidelights on the Prussian Guard'. *Tradition*, No. 66, pp 26–27; 33.

MARRION, R. W. 'British Field Service Uniforms – Sudan 1898'. *Tradition*, No. 19/Volume IV. pp 26–28; 30.

'Military Antiques, Some Imperial German Headdresses 1900–1914'. *Tradition*, No. 23/Volume IV. pp 28–29.

RIEHN, Richard K., 'A Helmet of the Saxon Gardereiter'. *The Soldier Shop Quarterly*, Vol. 15, No. 2. pp 1–3.

STACKE, Brevet-Major H. Fitzm., 'The Infantry Shako'. *Tradition*, No. 111/Volume II. pp 14–22.